A VISIONARY (
LUCID
DREAMING

"When you fall asleep at night, your mind doesn't just turn off like a light with the flick of a light switch. On the contrary, it enters a different and, at times, highly energetic mode of functioning. Lee Adams has written an excellent guide to exploring the dynamic powers and creative potentials of your own nocturnal brain. This book provides a wealth of detailed information and practical guidance for anyone interested in lucid dreams and the multiplicities of the dreaming imagination. Adams offers what few other writers about lucid dreaming are able to provide: a sensible and humble approach, grounded in empirical research, that encourages people to go beyond the mere attainment of lucidity to explore the deeper realms of the psyche."

KELLY BULKELEY, PH.D., DIRECTOR OF THE SLEEP
AND DREAM DATABASE AND AUTHOR OF
AN INTRODUCTION TO THE PSYCHOLOGY OF DREAMING

"This is the first book on lucid dreaming that not only covers the science and art of going lucid but also how to work with the deep mythological aspects of lucid dreams. It shows you how to have more lucid dreams and how to navigate them successfully as we consciously wake up to our own mythic lives."

RYAN HURD, DREAM AND SLEEP RESEARCHER AND
LECTURER IN HOLISTIC STUDIES AND PSYCHOLOGY
AT JOHN F. KENNEDY UNIVERSITY

"Lucid dreaming should no longer be seen as something esoteric, difficult, or available only to those with special talent. Astonishing adventures—hero journeys—are available to all of us on a nightly basis if we choose. *A Visionary Guide to Lucid Dreaming* is an accessible and entertaining resource with advice on everything from supplements that can help achieve lucidity to interpretive methods for working in and with the dream world."

ERIC WARGO, AUTHOR OF *PRECOGNITIVE DREAMWORK AND THE LONG SELF* AND *TIME LOOPS*

"This delightfully bold and truly unique guide is a powerful tool for both new and veteran mind explorers, offering ways to learn more about their nighttime adventures and themselves."

DAVID JAY BROWN, AUTHOR OF *DREAMING WIDE AWAKE*

A VISIONARY GUIDE TO
LUCID DREAMING

Methods for Working with the Deep Dream State

LEE ADAMS

Destiny Books

Rochester, Vermont

Destiny Books
One Park Street
Rochester, Vermont 05767
www.DestinyBooks.com

Text stock is SFI certified

Destiny Books is a division of Inner Traditions International

Cataloging-in-Publication Data for this title is available from the Library of Congress

ISBN 978-1-64411-237-3 (print)
ISBN 978-1-64411-238-0 (ebook)

Printed and bound in the United States by Lake Book Manufacturing, Inc. The text stock is SFI certified. The Sustainable Forestry Initiative® program promotes sustainable forest management.

10 9 8 7 6 5 4 3 2 1

Text design by Debbie Glogover and layout by Virginia Scott Bowman
This book was typeset in Garamond Premier Pro with Cocomat used as the display typeface
Illustrations by Oray Studios

To send correspondence to the author of this book, mail a first-class letter to the author c/o Inner Traditions • Bear & Company, One Park Street, Rochester, VT 05767, and we will forward the communication, or contact the author directly at **https://taileaters.com/lucid-dreaming-book**.

◆◆◆

This book is dedicated to all the lucid dreamers
and researchers who came before me.
Their work has enabled me to dive deeper
than I ever would have.

Contents

PART 3

Working with Your Dreams

PART 4

The Dreamer's Journey

PART 5

Advanced Tools and Supplements for Lucid Dreaming

Acknowledgments

This book is the natural result of many articles, blog posts, and studies I've done over the many years of my dream work so far. Taking that journey and documenting it would not have happened without the support of many people. First, thank you to my longtime friend and mentor Ryan Hurd, for helping me to understand dreams and their importance to my personal life. Huge thanks to my wife, Kristie, who has kept me grounded while I've explored my dreams and sometimes acted a little crazy. To my mother for helping me always know that dreams are important and to listen to their messages, regardless of how outlandish they seem. To my colleague and life coach Richard Guinn, for his help in teaching me the importance of self-discovery. I would like to thank my Buddhist teacher and friend Jay Feldman for being a wonderful help in accepting my shadow. I would like to thank Meg Ryan for her help in editing this book and turning it into something that could be readable and informative to all.

And importantly, thank you to the Taileaters online community. Your enthusiasm and contributions have inspired me, challenged me, and helped me to grow as a thinker, writer, and dreamer.

Join other oneironauts to talk about dreams and dreaming at taileaters.com/discussion.

An Invitation to the Hero's Journey

I met a guy who told me he was an exile transcendentally engaged with an alchemy of invisible worlds, too engrossed by far to remember his country, the ache of all he had to leave behind, enflamed nightly by his nameless supernals, enflamed nightly by his impossible task, and I thought why not?

—Darren Hughes, shared via
personal communication

I am a dreamer and have been all my life. I have always enjoyed having and discussing dreams and hearing about other people's amazing adventures. Throughout life, distractions and responsibilities naturally come up that have taken me away from my dream work, but I've always come back to it. Somehow, it feels as if something is missing from my life when I'm not paying attention to my dreams. To me, dreams feel essential, and listening to them is a spiritual practice.

Dreams can have extreme impacts on our lives if we choose to listen to them. Some dreams can make a major impact; they are often called big dreams because they make such a lasting impression. Understanding and incorporating these dreams into our daily lives, implementing the changes that they sometimes ask us to make, and sharing these experiences with others can ultimately change our sense of reality.

Perhaps like many of you, I've been able to lucid dream since I was quite young—I just didn't realize that was what it was. These dreams have ranged from minor experiences that last a few moments to experiences that go on for what seems like hours, from merely being aware that I am dreaming to having full-blown conversations with characters in my dreams or trying to control the physics of the dream environment.

When I was young, most of the people around me disregarded dreams as mental noise. However, my mother, who is a deeply religious person, explained to me that dreams played an important role in prophecy and encouraged me to look for meaning in mine. Still, I felt a disconnect between how important my dreams felt and any impact they might have on my waking life. I wanted to close that gap.

And yet, making that leap was a scary prospect, and my dreams told me as much. The first big dream I remember hinted at the task ahead of me:

I am walking through a college campus or schoolyard and see a large building. I become aware that I am dreaming when I recognize that the chapel I am looking at does not exist in the real world. I walk into the chapel, and it opens up into pews full of people working. I ask a few students what they're doing, and they respond that they are doing homework. They seem friendly and open to answering my questions.

This dream helped me to see that there is more going on behind the wakeful consciousness in the higher areas of the unconscious, which I call the Self.

It would be years before I fully accepted the challenge. I felt conflicted about incorporating the messages I felt my dreams were giving me. They didn't line up with my worldview at the time, which was a mixture of stubborn adherence to the scientific method and inherited monotheistic beliefs.

It wasn't until I dove into Jungian psychology and Joseph Campbell's work that I started to fully realize the similarity between my dream experiences and the themes and archetypes described by these two thinkers. Campbell's idea of the Hero's Journey accurately summarized my dream experiences. He calls the Hero's Journey "a magnification of the formula represented in the rites of passage: separation-initiation-return." His definition may be more simply described as an adventure on which the hero embarks. A crisis initiates the journey, then the Hero overcomes an adversary, and then he or she finally returns, changed in some way. Jung called this process individuation, by which he meant the complete actualization of the whole human being through bringing the conscious and the unconscious into balance.

After I understood my own dreams in terms of the individuation process, I began to see the anatomy of dreams and to navigate the map of the deeper levels of understanding dreams offer. As I released the desire to control the dream experience and instead allowed them to express naturally, I was able to start to face unknown fears, including death. This transformed my life in ways that no previous experience had.

As I've further explored my dreams and related my personal experiences to thousands of others, I've come to believe that all dreams contain an invitation and opportunity to take the Hero's Journey. While Campbell was describing a mythological journey that we are all taking during our waking life, we can make this journey much more personal in dreams, bringing about even greater transformation.

It's my hope that sharing part of my ongoing individuation process can not only provide you with an overview of the limitless variety of experiences available in the dream world, but also offer some encouragement—a traveling companion as you find new meaning in your dreams. And ultimately, I hope that you will discover your own Hero's Journey.

An Introduction to How to Use This Book

Most guides to deep dreaming and altered states focus on providing ways to have more of these experiences. That's understandable: lucid dreaming is elusive and fascinating, so it's natural to want to learn how to do it—and then to do it as much as possible. What those guides don't provide is what becomes available once you reach that level of awareness. My goal is to offer a guide to lucid dreaming techniques as well as a road map to the deeper transformation that lucid dreaming can bring. I share my personal experiences to show you that such transformation is possible and to serve as a guide.

In writing this book I hope to provide an easy-to-follow path to help you build your lucid dreaming skills and use dream work in your personal development and growth. This book is meant to provide you with a foundation of the science and techniques of lucid dreaming that can advance your practice, wherever you are, to dive more deeply and with more clarity and intentionality into your unconscious. It also provides a way for those veteran lucid dreamers to advance their practice.

The concepts and practices in this book are presented alongside examples of my own dreams and dream journaling. As I share how I've worked with particular dreams over time, I hope you'll gain a better understanding of how you can make lucid dreaming a habit and use it as a portal into your own explorations of the unconscious.

Lucid dreaming comes with challenges both physical and mental, many of which will be addressed in this book. They may include changing your sleep habits, taking supplements, or changing your worldview. It's important that you feel up to this challenge. That said, please be aware that the information and techniques in this book in no way constitute medical, psychological, or other clinical advice. Do not substitute anything in this book for the advice of a qualified medical or clinical professional.

If you feel at any time that you are being pushed too much, pause. This practice is meant to improve your life, but our readiness to engage in a potentially intense practice such as lucid dreaming can come and go. If now is your time, welcome. As you proceed, remember that the advice here is a suggestion only and is in no way prescriptive or required.

Exploring and altering your consciousness can become intense, so it's important to get some of the basic concepts about dreams and memory in hand before you dive in. Some of the experiences you'll have when lucid dreaming can be troubling and must be handled with care. The goal here is to enjoy this process, and that requires a bit of preparation, which I provide alongside some background on the physiology, history, and philosophy of dreaming, so that you can personalize your own well-rounded, grounded practice.

I want to emphasize that I don't believe there is any one right or wrong way to dream, to lucid dream, or to explore out-of-body sensations. I see all dreams as calling us to learn more about ourselves and to build a more complete understanding of who we are. Releasing control over the dream and having the willingness to listen to your dreams is the first step. Kelly Bulkeley wrote in his *Introduction to the Psychology of Dreaming* that dream work is an essential part of understanding the realm of consciousness that extends beyond the personal, to a place of appreciating universal experience and awareness. How you get there is somewhat secondary. You may use some of the same techniques that I have used, and you may bring in your own.

PART 1

•••

The Dreamer

and the

Dream

1
Why Lucid Dream?

WHAT IS LUCID DREAMING?

Lucid dreaming—the most basic definition being the act of dreaming while being aware that one is dreaming—has been around for a long time. The philosopher Aristotle wrote about lucid dreams in some of his writings, and other major philosophers have mentioned it as well. There is some interesting evidence that even the Egyptians may have performed some lucid dreaming techniques. In the Tibetan and Egyptian books of the dead we find evidence that lucid dreaming was used to actively prepare for death. We also know that lucid dreaming was used by ancient yogis to travel astrally, and that Buddhist monks have practiced dream yoga to access the inner self. Tenzin Wangyal Rinpoche's book *The Tibetan Yogas of Dream and Sleep* describes lucid dreaming as an active meditation practice as old as the Tibetan culture itself.

Even with its long history, lucid dreaming still wasn't taken seriously until scientific studies were conducted by Stephen LaBerge, one of the most well-known psychophysiologists to study lucid dreaming and to show the larger scientific community that lucid dreaming was in fact something people could do. In the twenty or so years since, more and more studies have been conducted on this altered state of consciousness. Today lucid dreaming is widely accepted, and the phenomenon has even been depicted by Hollywood in films such as *Inception* and *Vanilla Sky.*

WHY LUCID DREAM?

Why? Or more to the point, *why are we doing this?* The question seems almost banal, but it's one of the most important things to ask ourselves if we are to get the most out of a lucid dreaming practice. Ask *why* often enough, and we eventually get to the root desire that might have been hidden from our consciousness until now.

That is, in fact, exactly the reason to ask this deceptively important question. It helps us to dredge up whatever is lying beneath our awareness. In this way, it is the true beginning of a lucid dreaming practice—a practice that invites us deep into conscious and subconscious realms in order to deliver pieces of ourselves back to ourselves.

With lucid dreaming, having focus is key to success. Most of the skills needed to obtain lucidity in an altered state require you to pay attention to sensations, use those sensations to recognize the states of consciousness you find yourself in, and eventually control how you interact with those states. This all requires deep, clear focus. Articulating for yourself why you are doing this is the beginning of this kind of focus.

Whether you are new to lucid dreaming or have been practicing for a while, pause for a moment and consider: Why do you want to lucid dream? If you don't fully understand why you are seeking whatever it is you're seeking, then it becomes less likely that your dreaming will yield for you all the results and rewards that it can. Understanding your reasons for embarking on this journey will focus your path. Having a clear intention for your journey is another key to success.

Many superficial answers arise when you ask yourself *why,* and it's also important to explore these. Do you hope to obtain special abilities or powers? Ask yourself if you crave more excitement in your life. Maybe it would be more constructive to find motivation in improving your sense of self. Spend a significant deal of time understanding the *why* before you direct your attention to the reasons that come up.

Discovering your true desires and aligning them with a set of goals that will truly help you achieve them takes time and energy.

Why is also a dynamic question. The answer may change over time. The reasons, motivations, and desires that drive us today may lose their charge tomorrow, in a month, in a year, or in a decade. As we learn and grow, our *why* will change as surely as our lives, beliefs, and priorities change.

When I first started to explore lucid dreaming, I did it as a form of entertainment. If I had been asked as a twenty-year-old why I lucid dreamed, I would have said, "To have fun and to escape ordinary life." As I learned more about lucid dreaming, I started to realize that there was more to the dream world than I had expected. The lucid dream state became a way for me to communicate with a deeper part of the Self, and to better understand that Self and its dream world. I started dreaming to escape; I ended up dreaming to stay with myself and to become more whole.

2

What to Expect
in a Lucid Dream

Lucid dreams come with a variety of physical sensations. Sounds of rushing water, numbness on the lips, a feeling of being pushed down or of sinking into your bed, or even a sense of a presence observing you are all common and normal. One of the most common sensations is to feel vibrations—anything from a mild tingling to feeling a bit like your body is coming apart or dissolving. Though understandably alarming at first, these sensations are nothing to worry about: they mean you're becoming aware of the process of falling asleep, and they will pass as you relax. Consider the following dream experience I had:

Falling asleep, I feel the vibrations that normally come when I know I will have an out-of-body experience type dream. I open my eyes, and I'm in my room. Things seem slower, and I know that there is a good chance I am dreaming. I walk around my room and think that there is a chance that I am sleepwalking, as everything is very slow but still realistic. I fear my roommates will see me walking around the house but figure the risk is worth it and continue on my way to the bathroom to look in the mirror. . . .

Though prior to this I had had many lucid dreams, this example shows the level of realness that can be experienced in a lucid dream. The best way to prepare for experiences in lucid dreaming is to first expect the unexpected, and second, to practice being aware of whatever you experience. Both principles especially apply to physical sensations and surroundings. Compare the waking and dreaming versions of each.

UNDERSTANDING THE BODY

Some of the experiences around lucid dreaming can be scary and confusing, and they can cause a lucid dream to become negative or to end suddenly if the dream is poorly understood. If you can relax your body during these events, you can change the experience as well as the direction and results of the dream.

There are specific sensations that cue a lucid dream or out-of-body experience. Buzzing sounds are often heard before or during sleep paralysis and are a good indicator that a lucid dream or out-of-body experience is about to occur. Hypnotic hallucinations, paralysis, extreme vibrations, and a sense of floating or falling often are tied to these types of dreams as well. If you remind yourself that this is common, they will be less alarming should you experience them.

REALISM

When a person first starts to explore a lucid dream, they are often found testing the environment to see how real something is or is not. A normal lucid dream contains a type of realism that is below the realism of reality. There may be impossibilities in the physics of the dream world or unrealistic characters involved in the dream.

In cases where people have out-of-body-experience lucid dreams, the realism is increased to another level. In an out-of-body experience, there seems to be an even greater realization that they are dreaming or traveling to another level of reality. Details are more vivid in out-of-body experiences than they are in normal lucid dreams; out-of-body experiences often seem so real that many dreamers have believed that these dreams are, in fact, real 3D experiences.

Simple experiments within out-of-body experiences reveal that they pass standard reality checks in the dream, indicating they are more than just basic lucid dreams. I tested the reality of the following dream, which I introduced at the beginning of this chapter:

I flick on and off the light in the bathroom and it works as it should, which causes me to believe that I'm sleepwalking. I look at my face in the mirror and notice everything is slightly green. I walk down the stairs, which lead to outside the house, and see my shoes. I position my shoes so that when I awake the next day I will see that I was sleepwalking. I continue outside, where the sky is full of amazing stars and supernovas. After walking around for a while, I lose my lucidity and have a long dream. When I awake and check my shoes, I see that they are not positioned in any strange manner, and I notice that the temperature outside is around fifteen degrees, which would have caused me to wake up if I had gone outside in my sleeping clothes.

Although in this dream I thought the out-of-body experience was real, I still was unable to produce any results where the dream interacted with reality. Theories have been presented that when we have an out-of-body experience our minds tend to create a world that resembles the one we went to sleep in. Often there is a portal—literally, a door or window in the dream—that we walk (or run or fly) through to be transported into a unique dream world.

It is unknown exactly why these dreams seem so much more real than other types of lucid dreams, but it's hypothesized that the area of the brain that deals with long-term memory and intention remains active during the dream. Another hypothesis is that these dreams are interacting with another form or level of reality called the astral. Regardless of the reason, often people who have out-of-body experiences also feel vibrations, have auditory and visual hallucinations, and even have sleep paralysis.

3

Consciousness

The Route to "Beyond"

Being aware that one is dreaming while one is dreaming means many different things to many different people. Some call this experience a lucid dream.* If a dreamer reaches a certain quality of consciousness in the dream state, they may think of themselves as having had an out-of-body experience. Even beyond that, some would describe themselves as being conscious while traveling amid a mixture of realities, past the known sense of time, in an astral state. Where do waking reality, passive dreams, lucid dreams, out-of-body experiences, and astral projection begin and end?

To even approach these distinctions, we have to first wrap our minds around consciousness itself. What exactly *is* consciousness? How does it differ from what we call the mind? We need to at least get a basic grasp of these concepts before we can explore altered dream states in a meaningful way.

The study of consciousness is a recent development in the scientific community. Until only recently, consciousness has been a mystery,

---

*When it comes to consciousness, nothing is black and white. For this reason, and to simplify the discussion, this guide classifies a lucid dream as any dream in which the dreamer has any level of awareness that he or she is dreaming.

difficult to study in the same way that it would be difficult for a fish to understand water. Because we experience studying consciousness as thinking, we also tend to forget one of the key paradoxes about lucid dreaming and other paths to exploring the beyondness of mind: consciousness is, to a large extent, a physical phenomenon.

Consciousness expresses itself in awareness, alertness, attention, vigilance, focus, and wakefulness. We can experience these states internally, and no one person can experience them for anyone else. Their only external evidence is the behavior associated with them. For practical purposes, this is good enough.

The implication is pretty heavy, though: if consciousness is impossible to experience or prove externally, then I can only be truly certain about my own consciousness. It is impossible for me to be sure of anything more than that. I can't know that you, the reader, are conscious. I can only give you the benefit of the doubt.

Contemporary ideas about the origins of consciousness focus on the observer and the observed. Tony Nader, a neuroscientist, researcher, and leader in the Transcendental Meditation movement, posits that for something to be conscious, it must possess three basic qualities:

1. It must be able to observe.
2. It must have observed itself.
3. It must experience the process of observation.

It's basically a chicken and egg problem: in order to be conscious of myself, I must first be able to observe myself or my own awareness. However, I have to be aware in order to notice and observe my consciousness.

CONSCIOUSNESS IS PHYSICAL

Most philosophical and abstract approaches show us how consciousness plays out in the mind and in our environment. But these approaches only display how consciousness can express itself; the physical approach to understanding consciousness can teach us a great deal about how consciousness comes into being and what is logically required for consciousness to be experienced. The physiological and biological basis of consciousness grounds our understanding in ways that make both the fact of consciousness and the way we interact with it that much more remarkable.

It takes the human brain just 250 milliseconds to deliver a piece of sensory information to our awareness. It takes, on average, 30 to 50 milliseconds for stimuli to reach the brain and then 150 milliseconds of processing before reaching our awareness. This continuous triggering of synapses is what we experience as conscious awareness, or cognition. Whether this is the same as the "is-ness" we all experience as part of what we commonly understand as consciousness is a matter of debate among both philosophers and neuroscientists.

While this process appears to be automatic, and something we experience simply as what is, in reality what's going on behind the scenes is much more like a screen on a computer running at sixty frames per second and giving us the illusion that we are seeing a continuous image.

There is abundant evidence that consciousness is influenced by physical experiences. Changing how the body functions—what you eat, drink, and do with your body, as well as physical traumas, stress, and the natural processes of growth and aging—creates hormonal changes, which cause reactions in the mind, which we experience as consciousness.

This also works in the reverse: consciousness affects physical states. Change how you see, and the things you see change, as the saying goes. In many world traditions, historically and even to this day, it is believed that the process of change originates with the spirit and is processed in the mind, which then creates the reactions in the body. If we replace the word *spirit* with *consciousness,* we find the same is true today. Changes in consciousness, in turn, alter hormone balances in the brain, which then influence the body as a whole.

In a way, studying consciousness is like reading a map drawn with magic ink: shining a black light reveals the hidden image. Researchers can study consciousness using biological markers, such as the amount of oxygen being used by the brain. When the brain is using more oxygen in specific areas of the brain, it indicates that those areas are being activated. Through this analysis, researchers can see that specific areas of the brain are used in different tasks and that consciousness depends on many factors.

We can't see consciousness itself, but we can see neural activity and oxygen being utilized by the brain in ways indicating that what we refer to as consciousness is happening. As we identify patterns of neural activity, we can start to codify types of consciousness and understand what's happening to consciousness when part of the brain is modified, such as in an accident, during meditation, or when in a chemically altered state.

It's important to reiterate that consciousness doesn't mean the senses, the brain, or even a specific state of awareness; it is beyond those confines because outside factors, including the senses, our brain functions, and our mental states, can influence our level of awareness, or what we think or perceive in that awareness, as consciousness. We can alter consciousness based on how we interact with our senses, how the brain operates, or how we change our state of awareness, but consciousness is a thing in itself—self-contained as a state of awareness that's either on when you are aware or off when you are unaware.

Understanding how outside forces can change consciousness is just part of understanding how malleable it is. Consciousness changes based on how things are learned. When we first start learning a new topic or skill, we take in the new content pretty quickly. The learning is taking place in our conscious mind. Once we process that information, it gets stored as memory, which lives in the unconscious. We call this implicit cognition. Comprising knowledge, perception, or memory, implicit memory influences behavior and is outside of conscious awareness. A classic example of implicit cognition is the fact that we never forget how to ride a bike. The memory of the technique is somewhere in the back of the mind, so to speak, and the body's memory automatically comes to the fore when we start to ride.

STATES OF CONSCIOUSNESS

Consciousness can be broken into three states that are observable in all humans:

> **Waking:** You are awake, aware, moving around, and engaged in daily activities.
>
> **Dreaming:** You are most likely experiencing REM sleep and having a dream or some experience of simulated reality while sleeping.
>
> **Deep Sleep:** You are neither dreaming nor awake, and you are aware of thought. Sleep paralysis and many out-of-body experiences occur in deep sleep.

Within each of these states, impairment is possible, where consciousness is breaking down or operating improperly. This does not mean that the individual is conscious or unconscious; it just means that it's an altered form of consciousness functioning differently from what is expected when fully conscious. Here are a few examples of impaired states of consciousness:

> **Anesthesia:** A person is given a chemical compound that puts their body to sleep and temporarily disrupts their consciousness.
>
> **Locked-in State:** Complete paralysis of the body, rendering one unable to move. This makes the person feel imprisoned in their own body and closely describes sleep paralysis or other paralysis experiences in which a person is consciously aware during the experience.
>
> **Minimally Conscious State:** The mind goes through the normal cycles of waking, dreaming, and sleeping but is in an unresponsive state, although the brain will still respond to certain stimuli.
>
> **Vegetative State:** The individual is completely unresponsive (as when one is brain dead). Sleep in this state is not noticeably different from that of the waking state for the individual.
>
> **Coma:** The individual no longer experiences the waking, dreaming,

or sleep cycles. They are locked into one state of being, which is even more minimal than the minimally conscious state.

In addition to what most people would consider to be impaired states of consciousness, there are innumerable forms of altered states of consciousness that help define alternative ways awareness can be experienced. Some examples of experiences one might have when in certain altered states of consciousness include:

Drug-Induced Hallucinatory Experiences: Under the influence of certain hallucinogenic drugs, the functioning of the human brain can be altered in such a way as to produce various states of consciousness in which one's perceptions of reality, thought patterns, and emotions are radically altered relative to what one experiences when not under the influence of such drugs. This doesn't necessarily mean the user has lost conscious. In many cases, full conscious awareness can be maintained while using such substances.

Lucid Dreams: In the sleep state of consciousness, an individual can become aware that they are dreaming and become capable of exploring the dream as if they are awake and aware. (This doesn't always mean the dreamer will explore the dream, just that they could.)

Sleepwalking: Though not always remembered, the individual can be aware enough that they are able to move around while in a sleep state.

Hypnosis: Consciousness is altered to the point that the individual, while seemingly awake, is highly suggestible to outside influences.

As you can see, consciousness can change throughout the day; this is true not only for how much we are aware, but also for how we see our reality and interact with it on a fundamental level. Interestingly, our consciousness is directly linked to how our body reacts to the world around us, including our sleep cycle.

LEARNING AND
BRAIN CONSCIOUSNESS MODULATION

Specific areas of the brain perceive external stimuli, process that information, and provide us with a version of reality that makes sense to us. What we perceive as reality is nowhere close to what is real; rather, we see a tailored and processed representation of data. As discussed before, it can take up to one-fourth of a second before we are even consciously aware of what we are experiencing. Some areas of the brain first sense information before you are aware of or conscious of the information. Your awareness only occurs when a subsequent area of the brain becomes aware of the information.

The reticular formation is the part of the brain that regulates the amount of wakefulness you have. It also regulates consciousness, and damage to this area of the brain can result in coma. All sensory information goes to the reticular formation before being processed by any other areas of the brain. Other areas of the brain are responsible for highly specific aspects of consciousness. The hypothalamus controls the basic bodily functions of homeostasis. The midbrain and amygdala control the core self, or what we perceive as being the ego. The cortex is the autobiographical self, which contains language, speech, and memory.

Because it takes time for the brain to process all this information, and because this processing delays our sense of reality (even if only by milliseconds), the brain creates a masking effect to make a simulated continuous reality. In other words, the brain essentially makes up information that it is unable to obtain from our environment so that we have a continuous experience of consciousness. If an individual has specific diseases or lesions in the brain, he or she may experience a cinematographic version of time slowing and thus have moments of perception, rather than a continuous stream. Other contexts besides disease can create this loss of time due to the failure of the brain to maintain the continuous stream, such as the feeling, during a traumatic accident, of time slowing down.

Since the conscious experience that we have during the day is preprocessed by the unconscious parts of the brain (information that we are not yet aware of consciously), there is always an aspect of ourselves that we are unaware of—and this unconscious area controls a large portion of what we experience. These quirks of the brain come into play during lucid dreaming because we are actively trying to become aware that we are dreaming. But if the unconscious mind doesn't want us to be aware of the experiences in our dream, we never will. Most lucid dreaming techniques build a relationship with the unconscious so that we can become more aware of unconscious material in the dream state.

CONSCIOUSNESS IS PSYCHOSPIRITUAL

Having an ego or sense of self is another aspect of consciousness that occurs in the background. Though you may not often think about who you are or what represents you as a person, your conception of self is generated by consciousness. That same sense of self-generated consciousness shows up in the ways we define ourselves, such as identity, name, form, origin, nationality, status, or occupation.

Extending past the sense of self, actual consciousness is also an aspect of consciousness that is important to your overall view of reality. Actual consciousness includes your intentions, wishes, desires, emotions, thoughts, imaginings, and plans. These are the actions that are behind your consciousness, or how you play out what you desire the most. Unlike the sense of self, which is tied into who you are as an individual, actual consciousness is an expression of what the Self wants most.

Overall, the important thing is that your sense of self, or your ego, is not the whole you; it is a small part of who you are. You have aspects of yourself that you are unaware of that are essential in the dream experience. If you are aware of these unconscious aspects of yourself and able to build dialogue between those different facets, then you have a better chance of becoming aware of the larger sense of self in a dream experience. Allowing the unconscious to bring us into awareness within a dream is usually a far more effective approach than trying to force awareness into the dream. In the world of dreaming, the unconscious is in control. It is the unconscious that brings us to lucidity, which brings unconscious material into our conscious awareness—not the other way around.

CONSCIOUSNESS IS A PHILOSOPHY

Of course, the terms used to describe consciousness can change as others express their views of what consciousness is or is not, but overall, the ability to be awake, to be aware, and to evaluate the environment is a good summary of what it means to be conscious. It's important to understand that being able to evaluate the environment is a key aspect of consciousness, as I can unconsciously be aware of something without being able to evaluate it consciously.

Why does all of this matter? Because these concepts are keystones of lucid dreaming, and because consciousness is not the same as wakefulness, we can feel empowered to explore our dream worlds. If we can be aware, alert, and attentive while asleep, that awareness alone improves our capacity for lucid dreaming.

The unconscious, on the other hand, simply contains everything that we are not consciously aware of but which influences the conscious mind. Concepts such as forgotten memories and the earliest experiences that influence personality remain in the unconscious and are not normally available for inspection. We can access some of these memories through altering consciousness. This is why archetypal experiences often arise in dream states, during active imagination, and through hypnosis.*

> *The Unconscious is not unconscious; only the conscious is unconscious of what the unconscious is conscious of.*
>
> —FRANCES JEFFREY

---

*Archetypes are complexes or groups of emotions, patterns, and memories that extend past the individual personal experience. They are part of the collective unconscious, or the objective psyche, which includes the complexes that compose the entire human experience.

In other words—the unconscious is not itself unconscious—we're just not consciously aware of it. We can only know that there's something in us that we don't know. But just because we are unaware of something consciously doesn't mean that we are not equally or even more aware of it unconsciously. In fact, Carl G. Jung, a former student of Freud and ostensibly the first so-called depth psychologist, concluded that the unconscious was more aware and active in developing who we are. He believed that our conscious awareness as ego or the sense of self was a result of the unconscious expressing itself. Understanding that there is a part of us that is unconscious is an important part of exploring our dreams. Through dream experiences, we can bring that which is unconscious into our conscious mind. Through the processes of lucid dreaming and dream analysis, we can interact with our unconscious to learn more about our personal dream symbols and archetypes and explore their desires and needs. The ultimate result from interaction with these archetypes is an increase in awareness of the true Self.

One day we will understand how the brain identifies the world around us through interactions with our senses and complexes. New technologies are already helping us to understand what people are thinking without having to ask them. We can use brain patterns to figure out what is being processed inside the brain without talking to the individual. Positron emission tomography (the PET scan) is just one of the techniques being used to help us to identify these patterns. Though the technology is still quite primitive, it shows promise.

Ultimately, the big question of what actually makes something conscious troubles researchers. How can we re-create consciousness? How can we understand the subjective experiences that we have all the time? How do we make sense of our personal experience in relation to others? So far, no one has a good answer.

It does seem apparent, however, that subjective experience is where imagination resides. Imagination is what makes consciousness and self-awareness so powerful. Using the imagination to actively engage with the unconscious is what allows us to bring awareness to our dreams.

4

Awareness

Preparing to Dream

At first glance, you might think that lucid dreaming would be a simple skill to develop. To have a lucid dream, all we have to do is catch ourselves in the act of dreaming. How do we do this? Simply by noticing differences between the dream world and waking reality. However, for most people this is far easier said than done. Why? Because the state of awareness we typically find ourselves in during our dreams is one in which our ability to make rational observations of any kind is strongly curtailed relative to our normal waking state of awareness. As such, a key part of developing the skill of lucid dreaming is developing the habit of being as aware as possible during our waking hours.

It turns out that by increasing our waking level of awareness, we can also increase the level of awareness we experience during our dreams, thereby making it more likely that we'll be able to notice we're dreaming. Let's break this down.

WHAT IS AWARENESS?

Throughout my day I often catch myself zoning out. I can drive across town and end up at my destination without knowing how I got there or what was just playing on the radio. When this happens to me, it's because my mind has put itself into a trancelike state—in this case, to deal with the boredom of driving. However, you can zone out in response to any routine activity, especially any activity that you find routine or boring. All of us experience absentminded moments like this countless times every day.

It might sound alarming that we're all walking around in a trance at any given moment, but it has some perks. We don't have to focus on things we don't enjoy and can be somewhere else in our minds while we perform those tasks, we can escape and plan for things that are not right there in front of us, or we can have miniature adventures and fantasies while we zone out.

There are also some downsides to being in this state. For one, we are no longer paying attention. In addition to the obvious drawbacks— say, the risk of getting into an accident while driving—being in a trance makes us oblivious to much or all of whatever is happening in that moment. We dissociate from reality. While this can be a helpful coping mechanism in some cases, such as trauma, in everyday life these periods of desensitization, accumulated over time, can cause us to miss out on our lives.

Practices such as lucid dreaming and its supportive awareness practices help us to achieve the opposite of dissociation. We become more engaged, more awake, and more able to participate in our lives both while we are awake and while we're dreaming.

As we become more aware and engaged with our daily lives, our communication with our unconscious also improves. We may become more aware of the symbolic images and communications that appear to us from the unconscious. In the dream space the unconscious takes over, pushing our consciousness into a symbolic world that is generally unknown to us. If we do not become aware of this transition by practicing awareness training, we simply become engulfed by the unconscious world and forget that we are dreaming altogether.

MINDFULNESS

One of the most reliable methods for training the mind for lucid dreaming is practicing mindfulness. It's no coincidence that the world's most ancient lucid dreaming traditions, in Tibet and Egypt, also have some of the most profound mindfulness and meditation practices. This connection bears out in modern research: in one study of lucid dreamers, researchers found a positive correlation between those who could lucid dream and those who practiced mindfulness training.

Being aware means paying attention; that is, focusing on whatever you're immediately aware of in order to see what is truly there. Mindfulness training is exactly this. It is the practice of paying attention, opening your awareness to the present moment, even to things that may seem mundane, in order to see more clearly and to train the mind to be less reactive. The sensitivity that a mindfulness practice develops will improve your ability to be attentive to anything you choose.

Why Does Mindfulness Work?

Mindfulness training physically improves the connections within the brain. When we focus attention on a single object or concept, the brain adds neural connections to the areas of the brain corresponding to that object. The neurons' ability to change means that your brain improves its ability to process information relating to whatever it finds important. The brain is amazing in its adaptive ability, and this is just another instance of that.

Mindfulness can also have beneficial effects on the body. Your body is an electrical and chemical communication device. When your brain tells your body to move your foot or arm, electrical impulses are transferred via your nerves and then converted into chemical signals allowing those impulses to travel to other nerves. Eventually, these electrical and chemical signals translate into your moving a part of your body. The gaps between nerves can store chemicals, and some people have suggested these gaps are involved in the creation of memory. If that is the case, these gaps are also responsible for storing trauma, pain, and other ailments. When we focus on different areas of our bodies, we are directing electrical and chemical impulses to those areas to help improve the transfer of the signal while also improving the brain's awareness of those body parts. This can act as a release of that trauma or pain stored in your body.

HOW TO PRACTICE AWARENESS

In preparing to lucid dream, two methods of building awareness are particularly useful. One is mindfulness meditation; another is reality checks. Here's a quick introduction to both.

Mindfulness Meditation

In mindfulness meditation the goal is to produce no thoughts, so that energy normally used for busy thinking can be redirected toward awareness. Often people confuse the idea of no thoughts, which is commonly repeated as the goal of mindfulness meditation, to mean that you should restrict or push away thoughts. This is not the case. Mindfulness meditation asks us to allow thoughts to play out and be observed without attachment to any emotions that may arise in reaction to them. Practice nonattachment enough and your mind will learn that errant thoughts are not important, gradually becoming less preoccupied with mundane drama.

Traditionally, mindfulness meditation is done sitting down with your legs crossed and your back in a straight but relaxed position. The mental process consists of simply allowing your thoughts to play out while you observe them. It's important to remember not to force out your thoughts or to judge them (for example, classifying them as either bad or good). Just be aware of what you're thinking while allowing thoughts to freely come and go.

Reality Checks

You might think of reality checks as a basic form of lucid dreaming. Basically, you simply ask yourself if you're dreaming, but the practice involves a few steps.

First, become attentive to your surroundings. That means smelling the air, touching objects, and, especially, focusing on things in the real world that may appear different in the dream world. Examples of good objects to focus on are clocks, cell phones, and your hands.

Next, as you focus on whatever object you've chosen, look for anything about it that seems strange, while asking yourself, *Am I dreaming?* This process is like reciting a mantra, a repeating system of words that brings us awareness.

If you do reality checks like these often enough while you're awake, you may eventually find yourself looking closely at objects in dreams and asking yourself, *Am I dreaming?* just as you have been doing in the waking world. In dreams you will often find that objects you observe closely in this manner will have unusual properties—your hand may have seven fingers rather than five, for example—that will make you realize you're actually asleep and having a dream.

To improve on this technique, immediately after you wake up from a dream, identify the differences between waking reality and the dream. Think about what the surroundings, physical sensations, or sounds were like in the dream, and ask yourself how they compare with the real world. As you get into the habit of noticing how the dream world compares with waking reality, you can attain a higher level of awareness in both waking and dreaming states.

GETTING QUALITY REST

Everyone wants a good night's rest. Often, though, we wake exhausted. We didn't go to bed when we wanted to, we were up all night worrying, or we tossed and turned because of physical discomfort or pain. This impacts not only our day but also our ability to be aware in our dreams or to remember our dreams, two skills that are essential precursors to lucid dreaming. Getting a good night's rest is absolutely essential to lucid dreaming.

Effects of Poor Sleep

Sometimes the complications and stresses of life can interfere with getting quality rest. Sleep produces chemical changes in our brains that influence memory and cognition, as well as hormones that affect weight, diet, and mood. We will discuss these effects further when we talk about memory and dream recall in a later chapter. Even the United States military realizes the value of a good night's rest and makes it mandatory for American armed forces to have a given amount of time for sleep.

Improving Sleep: Firsthand Experience

I learned the effects of poor sleep—as well as techniques to improve sleep—in the military. I was working long hours on a Navy ship amid all kinds of chaos. Not only was the work stressful during the day, but a ship is also an extremely noisy environment, with machinery and personnel working around the clock. I would often wake up sometime between one and three a.m. to the noise of the ship's weapon systems, which were so loud that I could feel my chest vibrating.

In the Navy, a deployment can last up to twelve months. Sleeping poorly for this long can lead to some serious psychological and physical issues. Depression, aggression, and confusion, as well as weight gain, are just a few of the effects of disrupted sleep. A 2010 study by Ferdinand Zizi and his research partners shows that poor sleep may lead to an increased likelihood of diabetes. Getting the right amount and quality of rest is of absolute importance for a healthy mind and body.

Practicing good sleep is like learning a new instrument: it takes practice. If you have the patience and curiosity to discover the tools that work best for you, and the diligence to be consistent over time, your sleep will improve. You will feel more awake during the day, have a more consistent sleep habit, and improve your memory for both everyday living and your dreams. To develop those resources, it also helps to adopt habits that support healthy sleep throughout the day and at bedtime.

I learned some highly useful techniques that helped me while in the military and that have continued to help me while I apply them to my dream practice. They fall into three broad categories: daily habits such as exercise and nutrition, supplements as needed to support healthy relaxation and sleep, and a mindset of trust.

DAILY HABITS TO PROMOTE SLEEP

What kind of day will make you sleepy by the time evening comes around? One with plenty of physical exercise, balanced nutrition, challenging mental activity, and healthy management of emotions. Here are some of the tips I've learned, through trial and error, that may help you develop your own daily sleep-promoting habits.

Be Exhausted

As new parents, world travelers, or anyone in the military or a highly demanding job requiring long hours can tell you, being exhausted can get you to sleep fast! That is because stress can contribute to the loss of sleep, and getting daily exercise helps to reduce cortisol levels in the body, which in turn helps the body and mind relax, which helps you sleep better. Cortisol, known as the stress hormone, is directly related to our circadian rhythm functions and sleep regulation. Reducing how much cortisol is available during sleep will improve how quickly you get to sleep.

Exercise

A good workout, regardless of your level of fitness, can improve sleep by allowing your body and your brain to become physically exhausted. Working out is also a healthy stress reliever that can reduce how much you worry about your daily activities. There is a significant amount of scientific conversation currently taking place about how exercise affects sleep, but the consensus is that exercise helps you get to sleep faster and produces better sleep. I highly recommend light yoga before sleep because it involves stretching and deep breathing, which combine to help you relax and become sleepy.

Diet

It is well known that foods high in tryptophan, such as your Thanksgiving turkey, can promote sleep. This is because tryptophan increases levels of acetylcholine, a neurotransmitter important to sleep. Foods containing serotonin and gamma aminobutyric acid (GABA) also promote sleep. Examples of foods containing tryptophan, serotonin, and GABA are nuts, seeds, tofu, cheese, red meat, chicken, turkey, fish, oats, beans, lentils, and eggs. Eating more of these foods during the day, and also trying not to eat anything a few hours before going to bed, is a great way to promote sleep. Generally, eating healthy foods can contribute to quality sleep, too.

Being out in the field or on deployment with the military, I often didn't have the chance to eat the most healthful and delicious food or to choose what to eat. I had to make do with what I had while improving my sleep in other ways. Fortunately, I discovered vitamins and other supplements that could help make up the difference.

Supplements

Supplements are powerful tools to use in conjunction with other techniques that can assist you into becoming more aware during sleep. Some supplements support specific sleep stages that can allow you to get better rest, whereas others make it so that you are more awake and aware while sleeping, improving your chances of having a lucid dream. Though some individuals see supplements as cheating to achieve lucid states, supplements and herbs have been used by many traditions that use dreams as a spiritual and religious practice. Additionally, in today's world many foods lack the specific vitamins that are needed to support sleep naturally. With this in mind, supplements can assist your body in achieving natural dream states.

Melatonin is a tried-and-true sleep aid when it comes to helping me get to bed on time. Melatonin is a hormone naturally created in the brain. Taking it as a supplement can facilitate the process of falling asleep.

Niacin is my go-to supplement. It releases serotonin, as well as a protein called prostaglandin D2 (PGD2), considered to be a sleep modulator or activator that helps us fall sleep.

5-Hydroxytryptophan (5-HTP), closely related to serotonin, and **Saint John's Wort** are also excellent sleep aids. They act as mild antidepressants and help relax the mind in preparation for sleep.

The important thing to remember with supplements and vitamins is that you should only use them with your physician's approval, as some may be dangerous if used improperly. We will go into much greater detail about these and many other supplements in part 5.

Another way to help yourself get some good night's rest is to reduce the amount of **caffeine** you have during the day. I know that sounds like an impossible thing to do, but you can do it! When I was in the Navy, I managed to take a break from drinking coffee or energy drinks for a few months, which significantly improved my sleep quality and stamina.

A BEDTIME ROUTINE
TO PROMOTE GOOD SLEEP

Even if you've improved your chances for a good rest through your daily routine, the way you approach bedtime can make or break your success. It literally sets the stage for your dream time! Your external and internal environments need the sort of care that allows for a healthy sleep cycle and dreaming practice.

Create a Safe Sleep Space
(for Your Mind)

There is much debate about how the unconscious works and exactly what it is. Regardless of the ongoing scientific conversations, it would seem that our brains do have two different minds that are active in our lives. As previously discussed, the conscious mind is the mind we think with daily; it's also the identity that we think of when we think of our sense of self. The unconscious mind lies outside our everyday awareness and thinks pretty much about just one thing: survival. The unconscious wants to keep us physically safe and secure. As such, it draws our attention to whatever it believes will keep us alive and out of danger. Sometimes this means the unconscious keeps us awake when the conscious mind knows we should be sleeping.

Maybe you're stressed out, and your unconscious is perceiving a threat that it can't turn off. Maybe your imagination is telling you scary stories—playing the what-if game of possible futures, or being on guard for possible threats, imagined or real. When this happens, you won't be able to sleep well, if at all. Maybe you're not actively worrying about anything, but those same worries are running in the background—the unconscious doesn't differentiate. What's the solution?

How to Calm the Mind

The way to a calm mind is to not stay in a head space of maybes and what-ifs. When the unconscious starts sending you signals that it's in survival mode, it's time to talk yourself down, journal to get those thoughts out, and call lights out on a busy mind.

Meditation and Awareness Training

When we meditate, we see how thoughts and emotions are not usually as gravely important as they seem at first. Meditation allows us to detach ourselves from our thoughts, quiet our busy minds, and engage more effectively with life—which includes setting aside thoughts when it's time to sleep.

Have The Talk

When I lie down for the night and my mind is racing, I struggle with it for a while, and eventually I get fed up. That's when it's time to have The Talk. Addressing my own mind, I say (or write down) something like this: *You know how important it is to get good sleep. These things* that are bothering you right now—list those things—are important, too. However, they are not important right now. Can you fix them right now? No. You can fix them tomorrow; these all can wait, and we are perfectly safe until then. Right now, it is time for bed.

When you acknowledge your thoughts in this way, it helps the mind to calm down. In her book *The Dream Game*, Ann Faraday explains that the unconscious is unable to read our minds or to know what we are thinking. We must audibly say things or write things down for our unconscious to get the message.

The final part of The Talk makes a huge impact. When I say out loud, "It's time for bed," I often will immediately start to yawn and get tired, and soon after I will fall asleep. This conversation with yourself is a form of meditation, and a clearing of the mind is key to successful dreaming.

Create a Safe Sleep Space (for the Rest of You)

When getting ready for bed, we are setting the stage for our dream time. In a practical sense, this includes keeping your bedroom and bedding clean and calming. Keep the space as clutter-free as possible. Mindfully place items around the room that help you feel relaxed and happy. Without overwhelming the senses, surround yourself with textures and scents that relax you.

There's more to this than just making a pleasing aesthetic. Remember the unconscious? One of its goals is to keep you safe. A room full of clutter, stress, and chaos can put your brain on edge. Just watch an animal curl up for a nap: they smoosh and arrange their bedding until it's just right for them, so they feel protected and secure. There is a reason for that.

Turn Off the Lights

Put away your devices, too. Your nightlight may make you feel better if you have to get up in the middle of the night, but it's doing your sleep no favors. Even the slightest sliver of light can stop the brain's production of melatonin, its natural sleep aid. A purely dark room will do wonders for your sleep hygiene.

Better Sleep for Everyone

No matter what your job or lifestyle, where you live, or how much stress you're living with, you can improve your sleep. Does that mean these tools will lead to an absolutely ideal sleep situation? Not necessarily, but any improvement is a step in the right direction.

And take heart: I used these tools while I was on military deployment, and though I still had sleepless nights on occasion, for the most part I'd rate my sleep quality as above average. I greatly improved my ability to get a better night's rest.

I believe that you can, too.

5

Sleep Paralysis and Memory

The Obstacle Is the Gateway

I was living by myself in an old house in Virginia while working in the military, fixing aircraft on the graveyard shift. The stress of the constant work and the strange work schedule didn't allow for me to sleep as well as I would have liked. During the day, when I normally slept, my roommates would often make noises that would startle me awake. In one such case I thought my friend had jumped on my back and pinned me onto my bed. He then started to breathe in my ear, which upset and frightened me even more; I was unable to move under his incredible strength. The harder I tried to move, the harder he pushed me down and the more intense his breathing became.

Eventually I was able to break free, and in that instant I realized: I was alone. I had been asleep the whole time and imagined the whole thing.

This terrifying experience began my search to discover what had happened. After months of research and reading, I discovered what sleep paralysis was, why I was experiencing it, and how to manage it so I could stand up to my fears and regain power over my dreams.

Not to discourage anyone, but dreaming can be scary. Let's get the tough part out of the way first.

Many people who dive into lucid dreaming soon encounter emotionally troubling themes and images. To make matters worse, dreamers may often wake only to find these frightening images coincide with an alarming inability to move.

Sleep paralysis is such a common phenomenon among lucid dreamers that you owe it to yourself to find out about it before you dive in.

WHAT IS SLEEP PARALYSIS?

In his book *Sleep Paralysis: A Guide to Hypnagogic Visions and Visitors of the Night,* Ryan Hurd defines the state as a "harmless period of immobility, derived from muscle paralysis or atonia, [happening] every night as a natural side effect of dreaming sleep." Understanding sleep paralysis can relieve some of the anxiety you may experience when you go through it yourself.

Sleep paralysis happens when our bodies are going to sleep but we are still partially awake. This happens because of the brain's transition from rapid eye movement (REM) to non-rapid eye movement (NREM) sleep. During that transition, we are often still dreaming, yet are aware that the transition is happening. The result can be hallucinations that can range from unwelcome visitors to a feeling of being watched. Dreamers usually describe sleep paralysis as a combination of feeling paralyzed, sensing a presence, and seeing terrifying creatures.

Being paralyzed during sleep may be alarming, but it's natural. In a conversation with psychologist Rubin Naiman, Ph.D., a clinical assistant professor of medicine, as well as the sleep and dream specialist at the University of Arizona Andrew Weil Center for Integrative Medicine in Tucson, he assured me that "as frightening as [sleep paralysis] might be, it's perfectly safe." In fact, our bodies immobilize us during sleep so that we don't act out our dreams. Sleepwalking is an example of what can happen when this mechanism fails; however, sleep paralysis should not be feared. Research has traced sleepwalking to a part of the brain called the pons. Sam Kean explained: "Deep inside the reptile brain sits the pons, a hump in the brainstem an inch long. When we fall asleep, the pons initiates dreaming by sending signals through the mammal brain to the primate brain, where dreams stir to life. During dreams, the pons also dispatches a message to the spinal cord beneath it, which produces chemicals to make your muscles flaccid. This temporary paralysis prevents you from acting out nightmares by fleeing the bedroom or taking swings at werewolves."

During sleep paralysis, we can wake up and hallucinate images on top of our external environment. It's similar to an augmented reality of the brain.

Individuals report that sleep paralysis automatically instills a sense of dread regardless of what they see or experience. This may be due to a hyperactivation of the amygdala, the part of the brain considered to be the brain's fear center. Amygdala activation may be responsible for feeling troubled by nightmares in conjunction with sleep paralysis.

WAYS TO STOP SLEEP PARALYSIS

Researchers are still unsure why some people experience sleep paralysis and some don't. Where the research does essentially agree is that lucid dreaming techniques increase the likelihood that you will experience sleep paralysis. Some lucid dreaming techniques such as the Wake Back to Bed (WBTB) method and the Wake Induced Lucid Dreaming (WILD) technique (which we will talk about in later chapters) encourage the practitioner to feel the effects that resemble or mimic sleep paralysis.

While there is no known way to prevent sleep paralysis, there are a few things you can do to help reduce your risk of sleep paralysis:

- Don't sleep on your back.
- Sleep in familiar locations.
- Don't take naps during the day.
- Get exercise during the day.

- Avoid stress before going to bed.
- Avoid consuming stimulants before you sleep.
- Use a sleep mask to keep light from entering your eyes and help to keep your eyes closed.
- Get plenty of sleep every night.
- Eat a healthy diet.

If you do experience sleep paralysis, there are a few things you can do to break free:

- Wiggle your fingers and toes.
- Relax your mind.
- Breathe deeply.
- Close your eyes, and think about spinning.
- Talk to your doctor to rule out any health issues that may cause or exacerbate sleep paralysis.

Many of these techniques can be explored further in Ryan Hurd's book *Sleep Paralysis: A Guide to Hypnagogic Visions and Visitors of the Night,* a well-researched book on the subject of sleep paralysis.

THE POWER OF SLEEP PARALYSIS

The power of fear is strong. Fear makes us do amazing things, and it can also lead us to do terrifying things. Fear is used as a tool, a motivation, and even a weapon in the media, in marketing, and in war. To those exploring their consciousness, sleep paralysis allows us to come face-to-face with the most frightening experiences we can imagine. We can practice confronting and accepting those fears—and remove their power.

In the Tibetan Book of the Dead and the Egyptian Book of the Dead, this fear is described as the gatekeeper to the afterlife. Jung describes this same fear using the archetype of the shadow. Texts from traditions as diverse as alchemy, Freemasonry, and Christianity all talk about overcoming the shadow by facing fear in the archetype of death itself. Sleep paralysis can be disturbing, but to reap the benefits of lucid dreaming, it's a necessary risk.

SLEEP PARALYSIS
SEEN IN A DIFFERENT LIGHT

Accepting sleep paralysis is a large part of overcoming it. Accepting the unknown and that there are things we can't control is often enough to remove the fear. Sleep paralysis is a test to know whether we are ready and willing to move through fear and other aspects of ourselves that we don't want to see or feel the need to control.

Imagine seeing a scary movie for the first time, yet you magically know the entire movie, beginning to end. It wouldn't be nearly as scary; it may even ruin the fun. The same goes for sleep paralysis. If you accept that the experience is going to be strange, scary, and odd, you can neutralize some of the fear.

There's a deep life lesson in sleep paralysis, too. How often in life do we simply react before we understand what's actually happening? We do this out of fear or out of a reluctance to take in information we don't want to see or that we can't control. In sleep paralysis and lucid dreaming we practice being a mediator of the unfamiliar. The more we practice compassion toward ourselves during sleep, the more we're able to be compassionate during the rest of our lives.

Sleep paralysis provides a perfect opportunity to notice that you are aware while dreaming. Holding on to that awareness, you can jump-start the lucid dreaming process by allowing the dream to take place while simply observing it. Viewed in this light, sleep paralysis can be a key that both unlocks lucid dreaming and releases you from phantom fears.

MEMORY AND DREAM RECALL

The average person dreams four or five times each night and remembers one or two dreams. Not every dream is a long, cinematic story;

some are simply a brief sound or flash of light. But dreams they all are, nonetheless. We dream the most during REM sleep, but we may also dream during NREM, or non-REM, sleep. In his book *An Introduction to the Psychology of Dreaming,* Kelly Bulkeley explores NREM states in depth, including David Foulkes's work on identifying phenomena in NREM dreams, which are typically more bizarre, less story driven, and sometimes nightmarish.

Obviously, it's not having dreams that's challenging but remembering them.

In this chapter we explore some concepts about memory, how memory is formed in dreams, and how we can improve our ability to remember—all to increase our chances of becoming aware in our dreams and then remembering the experience later.

How we remember dreams is currently unknown. There are many theories, each contributing a different piece to the puzzle. If we look at them together, we can start to identify clues to how we are able to remember our dreams and then develop practices to support dream memory.

LONG-TERM POTENTIATION

To understand dream memory, it helps to understand how memory works in general. This process still isn't fully understood, but one popular theory involves the concept of long-term potentiation, or LTP. This occurs when synapses (these are the spaces that connect neurotransmitters in the brain) continue to fire over an extended period in a specific pattern. The continued activation creates a strengthening of that synapse to its neighboring synapses. This strengthening creates a memory. Inactivity of that synapse, on the other hand, can cause long-term depletion (LTD) and weaken the bonds between that synapse and those around it.

Because of the important role of LTD in long-term memory, most research into LTP has focused on the hippocampus as the seat of memory formation. Why does this matter to us dreamers? The hippocampus is essential to dreams because of its participation in converting short-term memories (the experience of the dream itself) into long-term memories in other regions of the brain so that when we wake, we can remember the dream. Specific neurotransmitters and hormones that the brain releases either allow for LTP or LTD in the hippocampus. Little is understood about these chemical processes; however, some recent work by Dr. Allan Hobson, a psychiatrist and dream researcher at Harvard Medical School, adds more clues to how dream memory works, which we'll outline next.

ACTIVATION-SYNTHESIS HYPOTHESIS

During REM sleep—the stage when we have the most dreams—there is an uptick of the protein acetylcholine in the brain. This chemical has a role in strengthening synapses. In Alzheimer's patients, for example, the breakdown of mechanisms that produce acetylcholine has been associated with memory loss. The increase of acetylcholine may be at least in part why we remember dreams.

This theory has its caveats, however. In a typical night we go through numerous sleep cycles, each of which lasts about ninety minutes and includes most or all of the sleep phases, including REM. This raises several questions: If we have several sleep phases each night, and REM happens in each phase, then why is it so hard to remember every REM phase? Why is it harder to remember dreams earlier in the night, or when we don't register being awake after a REM phase? It's not just about acetylcholine, then.

Though memory formation in dreams does increase in late night or early morning REM stages, this shows us that dreaming is yet a more complex process than simply the supply of acetylcholine in the brain.

Glutamate is another neurotransmitter being studied for its role in memory, particularly its relationship with Alzheimer's disease. This excitatory neurotransmitter acts in tandem with the depressant neurotransmitter GABA: when glutamate is active in the hippocampus, GABA is lowered. Studies have found that when substances such as those found in alcohol and marijuana bind to the GABA receptors in the hippocampus, we find an interesting result: the inability to form new memories. If we allow for these intoxicating substances to wear off, dream recall rebounds.

Acetylcholine and glutamate seem to be two of the heavy hitters when it comes to building new memories of all kinds. Further research points to hormones as another huge part of the equation.

Oxytocin:
The Pineal Gland Hormone
The pineal gland has a somewhat romantic association with dreaming and with altered or higher states of consciousness, thanks in part to its relationship to dimethyltryptamine (DMT), which has been found to naturally occur in the pineal gland of rats. Also referred to as the third eye, the pineal gland contains hormones that are involved in the sleep-wake cycle, specifically melatonin and vasotocin, or oxytocin. There is little research on oxytocin and its role in sleep per se, but it does have immense relevance for memory and dreams.

REM sleep is activated when melatonin releases oxytocin during sleep. Additionally, oxytocin is involved in the modulation of GABA and glutamate in the hippocampus, affecting the central nervous system. Melatonin is most active early in the night and declines as the night progresses and the pineal gland converts serotonin into melatonin. The balance of this oxytocin-melatonin-serotonin cocktail may contribute to the fluctuations in our ability to remember dreams.

Cortisol
Another contributing factor to memory recall that is often overlooked is the hormone cortisol. Like melatonin and oxytocin, cortisol also follows a circadian rhythm and is involved in memory formation in the hippocampus. High levels of cortisol can result in hippocampus dysfunction, which in turn can lead to memory issues.

A stress hormone, cortisol can be reduced with mindfulness meditation and exercise. Practices such as dream journaling, listening to binaural beats, and reality checks may also affect the cortisol levels in the hippocampus, which may be why these practices seem to improve dream recall.

A DREAM RECALL PILL?

Galantamine is a drug commonly prescribed to Alzheimer's patients to provide many of the compounds found to support memory. Studies dating back to 2006 have also established it as highly effective in dream memory formation and as a lucid dreaming supplement. Individuals taking it can become more aware of their dreams, control their dreams, and remember dreams after waking. Most researchers associate galantamine's ability to inhibit the enzyme acetylcholinesterase with why it is effective in its ability to improve memory recall. Acetylcholinesterase breaks down acetylcholine, and studies have shown that acetylcholine is directly related to memory recall in the brain, so the reduction of acetylcholinesterase may improve memory formation. Galantamine, however, also increases glutamate in the brain, which is also related to memory formation. This makes it a very powerful tool for memory improvement.

I have personally used galantamine and have had noticeable results. In chapter 29 we will look more closely at galantamine and its impacts, effects, and potential, but please know that it is important to consult your doctor or health professional before using any supplements to ensure that they are safe for you to use.

PART 2

•••

Lucid Dreaming:
Foundational
Techniques

6

Getting Past the Simulation

What does it mean to be aware that you are dreaming? Just as there are many levels of awareness, there are many levels to lucid dreaming. When you are in a dream, it's as if you are in a simulation, much like a video game, that is mimicking the reality you experience while awake. Most of the time, you aren't truly aware that you're in a simulation; you just passively experience the dream. In a lucid dream, you know you're in the simulation.

And just as with a video game, once you know you're working with a simulation, you can find the controls and learn how to operate them. With additional training and heightened awareness, you can eventually get past the simulation entirely and begin communicating directly with what Jung called the objective psyche.

This simple awareness that you are dreaming is the first stage of lucid dreaming. Continuing beyond that requires more work. This work has been described in the literature on Buddhist dream yoga, in Aristotle's description of being aware in dreams, in religious artwork promoted by the Catholic church, and now in contemporary scientific research. All of these sources have provided maps for getting past the unconscious self that creates the dream simulation and into an entirely different type of dream experience, one in which we can step into out-of-body experiences and astral projection. How far you take lucid dreaming, and the insights you derive from it, is up to you.

LEVELS OF LUCID DREAMS

Lucid dreaming can be broken into several categories or levels. Robert Waggoner, author of *Lucid Dreaming: Gateway to the Inner Self,* describes five stages of lucid dreaming.

Stage 1. Personal Play, Pleasure, and Pain Avoidance: In this stage, the individual who becomes lucid explores the lucid dream with a sense of awe by seeking out those things in the dream world that provide the most pleasure and avoiding anything that is troubling.

Stage 2. Manipulation, Movement, and Me: In this stage, the individual may be trying to explore the common lucid dreaming experience of being able to fly and may also manipulate the dream environment in other ways to achieve their ideal dream environment.

Stage 3. Power, Purpose, and Primacy: In this stage, the individual may realize that he or she has power over the dream characters and require that these characters obey the dreamer. The individual may also wonder about the purpose of the lucid dream and test different situations to determine that purpose.

Stage 4. Re-reflection, Reaching Out, and Wonder: In this stage, the individual may realize that the dream characters have something to offer the dreamer and ask the characters questions, looking for insight. Individuals may also ask questions that they know the answers to in order to better understand themselves and the dream world.

Stage 5. Experiencing Awareness: In this stage, the individual understands that something besides the egoic self is controlling the dream world. He or she goes past the images of the dream and seeks awareness behind the dream world. This is where out-of-body experiences and astral projection come into play.

The ultimate goal of a lucid dreamer can be said to be in stage 5 at all times, but often enough a single lucid dream can comprise many different stages of Waggoner's dreaming scale. It is not uncommon for a lucid dreamer who has been able to have a stage 5 lucid dream to go through other stages of lucid dreaming before experiencing another stage 5 lucid dream. I wouldn't get stuck on trying to have a stage 5 lucid dream all the time, as I don't think that is a realistic or positive goal. The important thing to know about these stages is simply that they exist. Let them inform your practice.

7

Let's Get Lucid

The Basics

t's usually fairly easy to have your first lucid dream. With a
reasonably healthy lifestyle and good bedtime routines, most
dreamers have success within a few nights.

And here's some even better news: there are almost as many lucid
dreaming techniques as there are dreamers, so if you hit an obstacle,
there are plenty more tools to try out. In this chapter we'll go over the
basics of how to lucid dream and then introduce some techniques to
support your dreaming practice.

Remember, lucid dreaming is an awareness practice. Anyone can
do it. You do not need to be a spiritual guru or achieve enlightenment
to do it (though if you do, more power to you). In fact, it's enough
to just believe that you can lucid dream and decide to start practicing. Sometimes simply immersing yourself in ideas about lucid dreaming, such as reading or talking about it, can increase your chances of
having lucid dreams.

There are countless guides promising lucid dreaming success. But
few agree on which practices are best, and even fewer are effective for
most people. The following suggestion provides seven simple steps to
begin your lucid dreaming adventure.

THE PROCESS:
SEVEN STEPS

The foundational lucid dreaming techniques revolve around good sleep hygiene and intention setting. Before you start pulling from a bigger bag of tricks, give this initial process time to work. You may be surprised at how the simple acts of noticing your surroundings, setting dream intentions, and supporting your sleep can ignite your mind's capacity to wake up to your own dreams.

These steps provide a simple framework for lucid dreaming. They fall into three categories: **before sleep, during sleep,** and **after dreaming.** Each group sets the stage for the next; it should take about two weeks of consistent practice for you to start seeing changes in your ability to be aware of and remember your dreams and to experience lucid dreaming.

BEFORE SLEEP

1. **Reality checks:** During your day, perform reality checks. Notice how things feel, how food tastes, how your hands look, how you interact with things, and so on. The reason for this is that in a dream we often notice something that doesn't fit with our view of reality or something that is out of place, such as gravity not working, a clock acting strangely, or even your hands looking odd. Identifying these errors can help us become lucid. Throughout the day ask yourself: "Am I dreaming?" Say it out loud if possible; take time to question this idea. Believe the question, and examine why you know you are awake. Use reality checks to test your waking environment to assist you in understanding if you are dreaming.

2. **Set the alarm:** Set your alarm to go off four to six hours after you go to sleep. We want your mind and body to be rested and to have gone through a few REM cycles before you even try to have a lucid dream. The more sleep cycles your body goes through, the

longer your REM cycles will be. Each sleep cycle is around ninety minutes. Because REM is associated with dreaming, the idea is that the longer your REM cycle is, the greater the chance to have a dream and to become lucid in it.

3. **Set your intention:** Tell yourself that you are going to have a lucid dream. Tell yourself that you will remember your dreams and that dreams are important to you.

During Sleep

4. **Wake up from the alarm:** When your alarm goes off, get up and go get some water, go to the bathroom, and do some activity for forty-five to sixty minutes, or whatever you feel comfortable with.

5. **Get ready to go back to sleep:** Lie down in bed and relax. Set the intention again that you are going to have a lucid dream.

6. **Go back to sleep:** This part is trickier, as you may be overstimulated at this point, and sleeping may be difficult. Just relax, and think about nothing. As you adopt this new sleep routine, your mind will automatically wake you up and allow you to go back to sleep pretty often. Every hour or so, your body will go through a phase of sleep, and you will wake back up. At this point, try your best not to open your eyes or move. You should notice that you're awake, but try to imagine seeing yourself in the mirror of your bathroom or imagine a face or object in your mind. If you can do that, then don't move your body, but imagine your body being able to move in your mind. If you move or nothing is working, that's okay. Luckily for you, you will have a number of tries before you wake up for the day. The main part of all this is to allow yourself to relax while also maintaining the self-determination to truly let the experience happen. It will happen! Additionally, if you did have a dream and remember it, actively focus on the dream; imagine yourself in that dream and what you would have done if you had been lucid in it. Think about that dream as if you

were lucid and set the intention to have a lucid dream while going back to bed.

After Dreaming

7. **Get involved:** Regardless of whether you have a lucid dream, getting into discussions with others about lucid dreaming will help you get to the next level.

8

Remembering
Your Dreams

As I mentioned earlier, the biggest takeaway, perhaps even the only takeaway, that is important in lucid dreaming is remembering your dreams. It's entirely possible that all of us have lucid dreams every night, but if a lucid dream falls in the waters of your unconscious and you aren't there to remember it . . .

According to Hobson (the Harvard dream researcher), the hippocampus, the area of the brain that controls long-term memory, shuts down while we dream. As a result, we may remember parts of our dreams while we are still sleeping, but we forget soon after we wake up. In the course of one night, we have a number of dreams, many of which we don't even realize we've had, precisely because of this shutting down.

A number of techniques have been created to circumvent this problem and to increase the chances of remembering dreams. Here, I've compiled, clarified, and expanded on most of these ideas, grading the techniques by complexity and type. The basics are outlined here, beginning with the easiest and ending with expert-level tools for those who don't mind sacrificing a little sleep for the sake of lucidity. We'll look even more closely at some of these techniques in the next chapters.

EASY

Explore Your Set and Setting

The term *set and setting* comes from the lexicon of psychoactive drugs, and oneirologists (those who study dreams) have adopted the term because the dream experience resembles a psychedelic trip. In *Dreaming Wide Awake: Lucid Dreaming, Shamanic Healing, and Psychedelics,* David Jay Brown delves into the relationship between lucid dreaming and psychedelics. In psychedelic research and literature, set and setting involves attending to your physical surroundings and creating a space that allows you to have a positive experience, and this concept could just as easily apply to lucid dreaming.

To examine your set and setting, look around your bedroom and notice the setting. Is it a sanctuary for sleep and dreaming? Or is it a mishmash of distracting objects? Remove clutter, electronic devices, or any other items that might distract your attention or irritate your senses. Keeping lights off will also help the photosensitive pineal gland to produce melatonin.

Set and setting includes how you arrange yourself in bed as well. Body position is associated with lucid dream quality: lying on your side may produce more typical dreams, while lying on your back may produce more out-of-body lucid dreams.

Keep a Dream Journal

Keeping a physical dream journal is perhaps the most important item in your lucid dreaming tool kit. Dream journals help keep our long-term memory active. Journaling also increases our motivation to remember dreams and increases our dream retention and recall after waking. The physical act of writing down words and images in a dream journal may also affect consciousness, since it requires an integrated act of mind, senses, and movement.

Wear a Sleep Mask

Unless you sleep in total darkness, a sleep mask is an essential tool for any dreaming practice. Sleep masks not only provide the darkness required for quality dreaming but also are a powerful reality check: if you know you went to sleep with a mask on and can suddenly see, then you know you are dreaming.

Meditation and Awareness

Being aware of your daily life is critical in becoming lucid. Paying attention to things that you are doing at any single moment creates a focus on the reality of the situation and allows you, when reality changes, to realize you are dreaming. Practice clearing the mind by focusing on breathing through a meditation practice. Focusing on an object or focusing on breathing while awake is one of the best ways to increase your dream recall and the likelihood of becoming lucid.

Be Aware of the Processes of Sleep

Understanding what your body does before it goes to sleep is an important way to recognize and maintain awareness as you fall asleep. Body twitches, temperature changes, and visual and auditory hallucinations are all common physiological responses as the body falls asleep. Practice noticing your unique process. As a complement to set and setting, you can also voluntarily twitch your body or induce a slightly lowered body temperature to trigger your body and mind's sleep and dreaming process. Lying on the back while practicing breathing techniques can enhance your awareness as well.

Use MILD

Mnemonic Induced Lucid Dreaming (MILD) is considered one of the most powerful ways to remember and improve your lucid dreaming ability. There have been many studies showing that the MILD technique is one of the best ways to improve your chances of having a lucid dream. Read more about MILD in chapter 9.

INTERMEDIATE

Wake Often

Waking up often may sound counterintuitive, but it is an effective way to teach the brain to toggle back and forth between being awake (the state most associated with awareness) and being asleep (the state most associated with dreaming). Waking up often can break apart the sleep cycle and cause your mind to be more aware while you should be sleeping. This will increase not only your dream recall but your overall control within your dreams.

Avoid Alcohol, Maybe

What you eat and drink can have important long- and short-term effects on your dreams. It's not uncommon for people to have a few drinks in the evening; the nightcap, often used to help relax and aid sleep, has become a bedtime trope. And there is some truth to the idea that drinking—even large amounts of alcohol—can result in an increase in the number of dreams you have and remember. It's a bit counterintuitive, because alcohol increases the amount of serotonin and GABA in your system—you may recall that serotonin blocks REM sleep and GABA reduces memory formation. However, once serotonin levels off, a REM rebound, a longer than normal REM period, follows. Similarly, once GABA drops off, long-term memory formation seems to be amplified.

While REM rebound sounds like an ideal state for remembering lucid dreams, the negative long-term health impact—including the depletion of serotonin over time that reduces overall sleep quality—probably outweighs the apparent immediate benefits of using alcohol to induce lucid dreams.

Increase Serotonin Naturally

Drinking milk or eating fish before bed will naturally increase serotonin levels and may trigger REM rebound. You can also take a supplements such as 5-HTP—a natural precursor to serotonin—before bed for similar effects.

EXPERT

Change the Sleep Cycle

Just as it's good to mix up your workouts when you are trying to build muscle, it's good to mix up the times you go to sleep to build lucid dreams. Your body and mind start to remember what time is normal to go to bed. If you mix up the times you go to bed and wake up, you can essentially trick the mind into thinking it should be awake when you are sleeping, bringing additional awareness to your dreams.

Consider Supplemental Support

In his book *Advanced Lucid Dreaming: The Power of Supplements,* Thomas Yuschak lists the supplements that he experimented with in order to increase his lucid dreaming. Broadly, this practice is known as Supplement Induced Lucid Dreaming (SILD), which uses nutritional supplements designed to reduce the amount of REM experienced during the first part of the night and extend REM to later in the sleep cycle. After some personal experimentation, I have found that the supplements most productive for lucid dreaming are those that support the production of acetylcholine, serotonin, and histamine.

> **Please use caution. Before using any supplements, consult your doctor or health professional to ensure that they are safe for you to use.**

Caffeine

Coffee and other caffeine-based stimulants contribute to the production of adrenaline and other chemicals—this is why many of us drink these beverages to perk up. When taken in small amounts, caffeine can actually help with becoming aware in sleep. Because caffeine acts as an antagonist to adenosine, it may help to convert serotonin into melatonin in the pineal gland. Taken to another level, the way you use caffeine can be used to elicit lucid dreams (see CWILD on the next page).

Caffeine-Withdrawal Induced
Lucid Dreaming (CWILD)

In this advanced technique, the dreamer uses caffeine until an addiction is formed (this sounds extreme, but the reality is that much of the world is already addicted to caffeine). Then you take the caffeine away suddenly, causing withdrawal symptoms to occur, and fall asleep. You're likely to wake up when you are in a REM cycle. The withdrawal symptoms go away and act as an indication to the dreamer that he or she is in a dream.

Serotonin

As discussed earlier, serotonin helps with reducing REM until later times in the sleep cycle and increasing the amount of dreams you remember. Serotonin also has benefits during the waking day: it's known to reduce depression, elevate mood, and reduce the desire to overeat. Using 5-HTP is a good way to increase serotonin production.

Acetylcholine

The neurotransmitter acetylcholine helps with memory and is tied directly to levels of wakefulness. Choline salts, which support the production of acetylcholine, can be used to increase the amount of acetylcholine in the body while sleeping. Acetylcholinesterase inhibitors such as galantamine can be particularly effective because they inhibit the normal breakdown of acetylcholine, allowing it to build up in the brain.

Histamines

Though histamines are seldom discussed in the lucid dreaming community, they may be, quite frankly, essential. Histamines are one of the easiest ways of releasing serotonin into the body. Histamines also can release a protein called PGD2, which is theorized to be the cause of sleep activation. Niacin, or vitamin B3, is a good supplement for this if you're willing to endure the niacin flush. As niacin releases serotonin and PGD2 into the body, it can produce a red flush or rash on the skin followed by tiredness and a sense of relaxation.

Timing

Having the right supplements seems to be half the battle; using them at the correct time is just as important. The best technique is the **Wake Back to Bed (WBTB)** method (see chapter 10).

Daytime: have some type of caffeinated drinks or supplements. This will produce a later withdrawal.

Daytime: don't use any caffeinated substances a day before you want to have a lucid dream or during any time period that would produce the withdrawal symptoms during sleep.

Bedtime: take a 5-HTP or a niacin supplement combination. This will increase the ability to have WILD dreams as well as allow you to remember your dreams later in the night after you wake up the second time.

Two Hours After Sleep: wake up and take a galantamine supplement along with a small amount of caffeine. This will increase memory and sleep cycle proficiency along with increasing the REM rebound about four hours into sleep.

Note: do *not* use this technique every night or on any night when you are not going to get more than six hours of sleep.

DAILY RITUAL

In order to get to the point of having lucid dreams regularly throughout your sleep, it's essential to set up a daily practice. This short guide will help you maintain consistency.

A. Supplements/Meditation: prior to sleep, take a supplement combination of niacin and 5-HTP. Relax in a meditative state with a breathing technique that allows you to be calm and ready for sleep.

B. After meditating, sleep.

C. After two hours of sleep, wake up. This allows the body to be rested and ready for the lucid dream. Waking up is also an opportunity to take the additional supplement, galantamine. Wait one hour, and then engage in your meditation practice to calm the mind and allow yourself to go back to sleep.

D. The relaxed state you will have achieved from meditation, the increase in REM sleep from the galantamine, and the reduced REM earlier in the night combine to make a WILD–type lucid dream likely at this point.

E. You can attempt more than one WILD dream by repeating steps C and D but without taking additional galantamine. This can be continued until you wake up to begin the next day.

F. After waking, write down your dreams in your journal, describing what you experienced that night as well as how you slept and what you'd like to improve on in the next night. This will help to reaffirm your lucid dreaming goals.

Perform additional meditation during the day not related to lucid dreaming, such as mindfulness, body awareness meditations, and yogic practices. Alternate between the days you perform the additional meditation practices and the lucid dreaming practices described in this book.

9

Lucid Dreaming the MILD Way

Now that you have a general overview of lucid dreaming, let's expand on some of the most profound techniques for achieving lucidity.

In the dream below, I had been practicing lucid dreaming for a few nights each week. This was my first night trying the Mnemonic Induced Lucid Dreaming, or MILD, technique. Though I didn't remain lucid for long, it was still a profound experience.

> *I am taking some college classes and having a hard time passing one of the courses. I typically have these dreams, as I am currently in school taking some classes that are a bit out of my comfort zone. At one point I know I am dreaming, and at that moment my whole body starts to float, and I am flying in the dream. I soon lose my attention, and the dream continues on.*

After this experience, I knew that the MILD technique, if used correctly, could be a powerful aid. In peer-reviewed research, Stephen LaBerge revealed that MILD not only effectively induces lucid dreams but also significantly improves dreamers' ability to lucid dream consistently.

The mnemonic technique is a popular memory tool you may recall from school. The reason it works is that it's easier for our minds to retrieve something that has been visualized than it is to retrieve information that is more complex and harder to visualize. It's why acronyms are easier to remember than long words. In lucid dreaming, we can use these same techniques, and I think of these as memory bridges—reference points that connect events in a dream to a familiar feeling, sound, or event related to it. These feelings, sounds, or events can be easily turned into visual memories.

In developing this method, LaBerge asked research participants to wake up during the night, recall their dream as it happened in their memories, and imagine what might have happened in the dream if they had been lucid. While focusing on that idea, participants would then go back to bed with the intention of having a lucid dream while simultaneously thinking about the past dream as if they had just had a lucid dream. This memory process created the mnemonic pattern that our brains so desire and in turn allowed dreamers to become lucid in their next dream.

HOW TO DO IT

Here's a rundown of the MILD technique for you to try:

1. Go to sleep while having the intention of having a lucid dream.
2. Wake up from the dream.
3. Imagine the dream you just had as if it was a lucid dream. Think about what you would have done had it been a lucid dream.
4. Go back to sleep while thinking about the previous dream as if it were a lucid dream and with the intention of having a lucid dream.

The most important factor for MILD is to recall the previous dream as if you had been lucid during it. Most people will discuss repeating the idea of having a lucid dream over and over before going to sleep. This is, however, not the most effective method, because it doesn't prime the brain in the way the MILD technique does. Having a connection to the dream you just had, imagining it to be lucid, and building a connection to the idea that lucidity is possible in the dream enables our brains to, in effect, remember to lucid dream. Put another way, we're coaching ourselves by asking, "If you could lucid dream, what would that dream have been like?"

It's easy to see why MILD works so well. The brain just had a dream in which we were not lucid, and we imagine ourselves as having a lucid dream; this sends the mind into a creative mode that is open to having the experience. Imagining having had a lucid dream pulls the lucid dream closer to us, letting our brains see that it's not only possible but easily within reach. Once we establish the memory-imagination relationship, we not only permit our minds to lucid dream, but give them the blueprint.

10

Wake Back to Bed

The **Wake Back to Bed (WBTB) method** is one of the most powerful lucid dreaming tools available. It provides the dreamer time to get enough solid rest while he or she is initially asleep and then jump directly into a lucid dream after going back to bed.

Whether we are asleep or awake, our bodies and minds follow a rhythm. Hormone production, neurotransmitters, and bodily functions, all of which control our conscious awareness level throughout the day, also fluctuate during sleep due to the wavelike pattern that we each experience known as circadian rhythm. While dreaming, our circadian rhythm follows a sleep cycle that lasts about ninety minutes. This sleep cycle can be extended depending on how many sleep cycles you can complete in the night. The longer you can extend these sleep cycles, the more time you have in REM, and the more dreams you are likely to remember.

Sleep cycles are also tied to the production of specific hormones and neurotransmitters that are responsible for the mechanism that produces dreams. Though we don't fully understand where dreams reside, or why we dream, we do understand some of the chemical processes required to make dreams appear.

When we allow our bodies to experience a few sleep cycles during the night, our minds become more accepting of the dreams that we are

60

experiencing. As we've discussed, the production of acetylcholine and the release of GABA during the dreaming process helps us raise our awareness levels as the night continues. This process helps deplete our reserves of memory-reducing serotonin, GABA, and oxytocin, the levels of which are highest during sleep. The WBTB method comes into action after we have completed a few sleep cycles and allowed our brains to support the depletion of these memory-fogging chemicals. This depletion allows us to be at the optimal levels to remember our dreams and to become aware of the dream itself, most likely by modulating the Default Mode Network to be more active. The Default Mode Network, or DMN as it's commonly known, is the default system that the brain uses in order to operate as normal while awake and vigilant. Any altering of this system leads to cognitive changes. Failure of the DMN can been seen in patients who suffer from dementia.

Not only are we allowing our sleep cycles to take place before attempting to become lucid, but we are also physically waking up, which cues the body and mind to start getting ready for the day. These additional processes increase awareness and memory formation. The WBTB method is a simple technique that allows you, to an extent, to orchestrate the sleep cycle and its normal chemical processes.

The Wake Back to Bed (WBTB) Method
1. Go to sleep and sleep for four to five hours.
2. Wake up with an alarm, and stay awake for thirty to sixty minutes.
3. Set your intention to have a lucid dream.
4. Go back to bed.
5. Get lucid!

When practicing WBTB, it's important to get good rest before waking up. That is why I recommend a good four to five hours of sleep first. This will allow for a few sleep cycles to happen before the alarm goes off.

What do you do when you wake up? This is a critical piece of the technique. Once you're awake, make sure you become fully awake before going back to sleep. Get out of bed, engage in some activity, and be aware of what is around you. Some physical exercise is a good option, as it releases adrenaline, which supports awareness while awake.

After about an hour of being awake and before going back to bed, set your intention of having a lucid dream. I encourage you to focus on one key element that you want to achieve while being lucid and focus on that idea while lying down and going back to bed. Your mind may be a bit more active at this time than you are used to while going to sleep, but with some practice, you will be able to go back to sleep after a few minutes.

A variation on WBTB that you can add to your tool kit is the Cycle Adjustment Technique (CAT), developed by Daniel Love. Much like WBTB, the objective of this technique is to disrupt the body's normal circadian rhythm cycle. Instead of setting an alarm and waking up, you go to sleep at different times each night, in effect tricking the body into more REM sleep.

11

WILDing

Extended Techniques and Lucid States

One of the most rewarding ways to have a lucid dream is through the Wake Induced Lucid Dreams (WILD) technique. Using WILD, you'll fall asleep while conscious and transport your active awareness into a dream state. Though this may be challenging, it is the surest way to become aware in a dream. You are essentially staying aware while falling asleep so that you do not become unconscious through the transition. You are staying aware through the whole process.

THE CHALLENGE

Most people who are trying to implement this technique understand the fundamental processes that are going to take place but are unable to reach the level of relaxation that tricks the body into thinking that they are asleep while remaining aware.

Our bodies and minds do their best to make sure that we are asleep before we dream in order to ensure that we don't start to dream while we are awake. Being awake while dreaming is basically a waking hallucination, and our survival instincts naturally prevent this.

When we lie down to sleep, our brains perform a series of tests to see if we are asleep. If we are aware of or awake for these tests, they can be disorienting or irritating. People feel the sense of falling as one of the body's first necessary tests, which is why we call the process of going to sleep falling asleep. Often people feel itching, warmth, or even electrical-type shocks passing over their bodies. Sometimes people hear buzzing or electrical sounds, which can be irritating. In these instances, our bodies are trying to have us respond to these sensations by making us move or respond. If we do not move, our bodies assume we are asleep. That's the trick to staying aware: being awake but not responding to these sensations will result in your falling asleep while aware, and that is what we want in order to achieve lucidity with this method.

Another significant challenge with the WILD technique is resisting the constant thoughts that float around our minds. It is essential to focus on the black space behind your eyes and not pay attention to anything else. Concentrating on nothingness is a form of meditation and relaxation that takes practice. It will be easier if you've been practicing mindfulness and meditation as discussed in part 1.

The last challenge in exploring the WILD technique is falling asleep unconsciously. If we are too tired or our bodies are too relaxed, we can fall asleep without awareness and lose the ability to be lucid in the dream space. The best way to fight this is to get rest before trying to attempt a WILD and to make sure to be just uncomfortable enough that you don't fall asleep too quickly. Sitting in a chair while trying a WILD may fight a tendency to fall asleep too swiftly. Attempting a WILD during the daytime, when you are naturally more alert, can also help you overcome these issues.

THE TECHNIQUE

THE WAKE INDUCED LUCID DREAMING TECHNIQUE

1. Sleep for five to six hours. Get solid rest, and don't try to perform any techniques before this initial sleep.

2. Wake up and do an activity for five to thirty minutes.
3. Settle back down in an upright or slightly uncomfortable position.
4. Close your eyes and focus on the blackness that you can see behind your closed eyelids. If images appear, do not force away those images.
5. Do your best not to move.
6. Do not react to any of the sensations you may feel.
7. Relax all parts of your body, from your toes to your head.
8. Breathe slowly and calmly.

After twenty to forty-five minutes of practicing these steps you should feel a slight change in your perception. A change in your awareness is the first step to an altered state and indicates you are on the right path. Have patience; daily practice is key to this technique. Often this change in consciousness is followed by the sensation of heaviness, your arms and legs twisting and turning, or ringing or popping sounds in your ears.

Depending on your ability to relax and perform the WILD method, within one to two hours you should feel a sensation of falling or of sleep paralysis.

SLEEP PARALYSIS AND THE VOID STATE

As discussed earlier, sleep paralysis is the inability to move while aware and asleep. You may see or hear strange and disorienting hallucinations during this period. Paralysis during sleep is the body's natural way to make sure we do not act out our dreams.

Most people do not experience sleep paralysis consciously, as they are typically asleep when it's happening. But because you are aware during WILD, there is the strong possibility that you will experience some sleep paralysis.

If you experience sleep paralysis during WILD, the best course of action is to continue to relax; do not fight the experience, however strange or frightening it may feel. The paralysis will pass, and you soon will fall into a void state.

Once you are in the void state, you may soon start to see a light or objects in your view. At this point, it may seem as if you are awake, as the sensations you feel and the things you see may seem completely realistic. Know and take comfort that you are most likely asleep.

At this point, try to do something that you typically could not, such as walk through a wall, float around your room, or fly from one room to the next. If you can perform any of these, you are now lucid in a dream state and ready to continue with your lucid dream.

ACTIVE IMAGINATION

Useful in conjunction with WBTB or WILD techniques, active imagination is a technique that draws the dream to the dreamer rather than the dreamer chasing after the dream. Jung and his students endorsed the practice but also warned of its intensity. It's been adopted in lucid dreaming communities more recently because it combines deep relaxation and imaginal practices—both known to encourage lucid dreams.

To practice active imagination, simply relax the mind without focusing on any specific thoughts that may arise. Hypnagogic visuals and imagery may start to appear, at which point you allow the imagery to intensify and engage with it as if you are communicating with another aspect of yourself. The key principle of active imagination is to follow the images where they arise rather than trying to pursue or manipulate them.

This is harder than it sounds. Often when we see something, we like to focus on it right away and force the content in the direction we desire. In this stage of sleep, the images will evaporate if you try that. However, if you can ignore the images, they will often intensify on their own; engaging at that point will allow the imagery to expand into a drama that you can observe in full awareness.

If hypnagogic images don't come to you easily, you can imagine yourself walking through your home or other familiar place. Think of the objects in that space, then add in some new features. This may jump-start the imagination and pull images up from your unconscious. With practice, this should lead to sleep while leaving the bridge between consciousness and unconsciousness connected.

12

Reality Checks

Are You Awake?

Reality checks apply mindfulness training to lucid dreaming. They are also the key to being a successful lucid dreamer.

In the lucid dreaming community, we call mindfulness training reality checks because the difference between lucid dreaming and reality is noticeable. By paying attention to reality, we can notice the sense of realism that is part of our waking life, and when we dream we notice the errors in the dream world. This results in the dreamer's becoming aware in the dream.

We already have assumed that reality itself is a simulation inside our brains. Our brains take in information using our five senses and mix all this information together in our minds—creating our impressions and beliefs about the world. Because both dreams and reality are simulated in our minds, dreams can feel just as real as reality.

Reality checks are also closely related to the Eastern practice of dream yoga. Dreamers are trying to wake themselves up in a lucid dream during sleep, while yogis are trying to wake themselves up from the dream of reality. Many yoga practitioners will say that sounds, visual indicators, psychological symbolism, and a physical practice all support them on their journey to enlightenment.

It's not fully understood how we can find errors in a dream by reality checking them, but it does work. Practicing mindfulness primes our brains to be more awake to our dreams and to remember them.

HOW TO PERFORM REALITY CHECKS

Here are just a few ways that you can practice reality checks throughout the day. It's important to remember that any one of these can fail to bring you awareness in a dream, so it's important to practice a few different reality check techniques.

- Look at your hands throughout the day, asking yourself whether you are dreaming.
- Focus on an object from your daily life to see whether that object appears in your dreams.
- Watch a clock during the day, and ask whether you are lucid dreaming.
- Practice meditation techniques throughout the day to help you focus and become more aware.

You can also make your own tools for reality checks by using sounds, lights, smells—anything that will allow you to recognize whether you are dreaming.

Having physical objects to check throughout the day can greatly improve the ability to become lucid during a dream. This often means holding something in your hand at several points throughout the day and asking yourself, "Am I dreaming?" This provides you with the visual (symbolic), physical, and psychological aspects of the practice. Verbally asking yourself if you are dreaming is an auditory cue, much like a mantra in yoga, to help remind your brain that it's important to focus on dreaming. Practicing these key elements will help you to become more aware throughout your day and while you are dreaming.

On your journey to a lucid dream, you will see that waking life and the dream life are closely related; one will teach you the importance of the other. Through mindfulness training in our waking life, we will see our dreams for what they are: a story. Eventually, we will see that our waking life is also a story.

THE POWER OF EMOTIONAL ENERGY

Using emotions such as fear, love, passion, or anger can allow us to become aware in our dreams. Identifying which emotion may be most useful to you is easy to do: think about the past dreams you have had and the overall emotional energy in those dreams. Once you identify that emotion, focus on it throughout the day. What thoughts are most vivid when that emotion arises?

Before going to bed, focus on that emotional energy and recognize that when you next feel it arise, you will be in a dream. This is a very useful reality check and can be extremely powerful to use in lucid dreaming.

For me, at one time many of my dreams were fear based. I knew that if I felt a lot of fighting energy, I was most likely in a dream. Before going to bed I would even psych myself up to the point that I would be emotionally empowered by the fear. That mental connection would allow me to become aware in the dream and even overcome my fear. As I started overcoming my response to fear, passion and love took its place.

Try using one form of emotional energy for this technique until it becomes useful in the dream, and use it until it is no longer effective.

13

Out-of-Body Experiences

Stepping into New Awareness

ut-of-body experiences are described as exactly that: individuals experience themselves stepping out of, floating over, or otherwise exiting their bodies. Most often, out-of-body experiences take place just after going to sleep because they are associated with the NREM sleep phase, which can cause dreaming and wakefulness to happen at the same time.

The reason you may experience the sensation of leaving your body in a lucid dream is that your brain still thinks you're awake, but your brain also has a copy of your body in the dream simulation. Your brain doesn't understand that you are in fact asleep. Dreamers experience a kind of dual awareness in which they can feel and sense things in the dream world while they also feel and sense things in the waking world as they lie in bed. Of course, this is just one explanation for out-of-body experiences; there are many that you can read about and explore to come up with a conclusion of your own.

Astral projection is taking the out-of-body experience of lucid dreaming to a deeper level. Often people describe that in their astral experiences, they have the ability to travel to other worlds or the land of the dead or to learn from the Akashic Records. I have also experienced this and can honestly say that it's breathtaking.

Though there may seem to be differences in states between a lucid dream, an out-of-body experience, and an astral projection, they are all part of the same process. When we are in one of these states of awareness, we are sensing differences based on our shifting of awareness from one state to another. In truth, they are all happening simultaneously. This would mean that we are dreaming, traveling out of our bodies in the astral realm, and awake all at the same time—in fact, what is changing is our shifting awareness, not our consciousness nor the realm in which we imagine ourselves.

For me, having out-of-body experiences is not completely reliable. Some days I'm more successful than I am on others. Sometimes I have lucid dreams without having the experience of leaving my body. On other days, I transition from a lucid dream into an out-of-body experience. Each person's experience is personal, and that requires us all to do our own work and understand ourselves—what factors seem to support each type of dreaming experience—in order to feel successful in our out-of-body experiences.

This chapter takes a practical approach and is generalized enough that each key point will contribute to your success in moving through these states. These tools are based on many people's trials and errors as well as research conducted in the fields of neuroscience and sleep science. There may be additional steps (that you won't find in this guide) that help you improve your chances of having an out-of-body experience, but those tactics are specific to you and will likely change over time.

WHY BOTHER?

A family member recently asked me why I would want to have an out-of-body experience. I related it to a familiar experience: how it feels to travel to a new country and explore, and how that visit may change us. People who travel know that it can be transformational; they want to discuss the upcoming trip, they want to learn about the culture and try new foods, and they want to explore. The same is true with an out-of-body experience.

Out-of-body experiences allow us to look at ourselves and reality in a new way. They allow us to peek inside of everything we know and see something more. It's an exploration of the soul and mind at the same time, a connection to the unknown. This may be the highest level of exploration, a true personal adventure. Out-of-body experiences also offer lessons about reality and our own psychology. With all that out-of-body experiences offer, who wouldn't want to do this?

The important question to ask yourself before you start on your practice is the same as for lucid dreaming: *Why?* Why do you truly want to have an out-of-body experience? What drove you in this direction? The more honest with yourself you are, the easier it will be to start to practice and the more likely it is that you will have success. Honesty now will lead to better out-of-body experiences later.

WHAT WAS THAT?

When I had my first out-of-body experience nearly fifteen years ago, my first thought was, *What was that?*

I didn't even know that out-of-body experiences were possible, and I was pretty confused. I had had many lucid dreams before my first out-of-body experience, but that first experience still totally changed my life. The main questions I asked myself at the time were:

1. What was the experience I just had?
2. Was the experience real?
3. How do I have that experience again?
4. When I do have that experience again, how can I control it?

SIX-STEP
PROCESS FOR SUCCESS

In previous chapters, we have reviewed many ways to experience lucid dreams. Now let's approach how to have the experience of being out of your body. What we want to focus on here is how to repeat an out-of-body experience with as high a success rate as possible. We use a simple six-step process with these elements in mind:

1. Set a strong intention to have the experience.
2. Get good rest.
3. Wake up and go back to bed.
4. Strengthen the intention again.
5. Go back to sleep.
6. Exit the body.

Step One: Set a Strong Intention

The most important thing you can possibly do in order to have any type of dream experience, be it lucid dreaming or an out-of-body experience, is setting the intention. This one attitude shift is key to training your mind to notice the effects of an out-of-body experience and reminding you that this experience is important to you. Additionally, focusing on the idea that dreams are important allows the mind to see reality in another light.

We find an exemplar of valuing the dream experience in Tibetan dream yoga. The importance of these experiences in Tibetan Buddhism seems to affect not only people's ability to have out-of-body experiences but is also at the root of the concept that all things are experienced first in the mind. Everything we do, think, and feel—all forming a shared reality—is simulated in the mind as we take information into the dynamic system of the mind, which in turn creates a dynamic virtual world that is then projected into the dynamic system of reality. Tibetan dream yoga works with this concept, playing with the malleability of thoughts and dreams. Jung suggested that, considering their extreme plasticity, memories and thoughts about those memories are actually fictitious versions of our own consciousness. Dreams, then, are more closely related to reality than we might think. Perhaps we should place more importance on dreams and less on what we deem real.

With that in mind, set your intention to be strong. Think that tonight you will have an out-of-body experience and that tonight you will remember it. Think about why you want to have an out-of-body experience and what one specific thing you would like to do during the out-of-body experience. Make this one thing easy to remember, with perhaps just a word to represent it, so that when you are there you can easily recall what it was you wanted to do. At this point, it's important to firmly believe that you will have an out-of-body experience and that you have no doubt that it will happen. This belief may be all you need to take the next step!

Step Two: Get Good Rest

This next step is easy. Go to sleep. Getting five to six hours of good rest each night is key to successful—or possibly any—lucid dreaming. Remember, you must achieve some quality rest before attempting to break yourself out of a sleep cycle. A well-rested brain and body are crucial for staying awake, staying aware, and being fully present when the time comes to experience the out-of-body experience.

Step Three: Wake Back to Bed

When you wake up after sleeping for those five or six hours (you might want to use a vibrating alarm to wake more gently and not disturb any sleepers nearby), you should be pretty groggy. That's why I suggest you get up for no less than forty-five minutes: you want your brain to wake up to the point that it thinks it's time to be active. As you become more awake and aware, the more conscious control you're likely to have as you trick your brain into going back to sleep. Use this time to write some emails, read, or do easy exercise. The more active, the better the results.

Step Four: Strengthen Your Intention

As in step one, reaffirm your intentions for an out-of-body experience. Think about what it may feel like or what you expect to see. Keep your mind open, and keep the thoughts easy and clear.

Step Five: Go Back to Sleep

Lie down and relax. It may be hard to go back to sleep at this point due to all the activity. That is perfectly normal. This active mind will allow for active memories. If you can lie still and not focus on your internal dialogue, you should start to see hypnagogic images (although if you don't, that's okay, too). This means your brain is doing its job and you are almost asleep. If you focus long enough, you should encounter vibrations, ringing in your ears, or sensations such as falling or floating. Do not focus on these sensations too much, as they are just distractions; keep relaxing until you are asleep (but still aware).

Step Six: Exit the Body

Once you are asleep and aware, you may find yourself in an odd state. Sometimes this can be tricky because our brains are masters at making us feel as if we are awake and that we have failed in our attempt. You might even have the sense of getting out of bed at this point, but in fact, you are having a false awakening and are in an out-of-body experience state already. If this happens, the thing to do is to take control of the out-of-body experience and exit the body.

Sensations

You may experience other sensations at this time, too, such as feeling locked into your body or having a shadow figure or presence in the room—in other words, sleep paralysis. Though this can be scary, remember this is perfectly normal. Additionally, the concept of a shadow figure or being pushed down or held down into your bed is often an effect of the brain being confused about your physical body and your astral body separating. Simply ignore these feelings; allow yourself to relax and think about floating a distance away from your body. This should relieve any frightening sensations and allow you to continue on with your exploration.

Use Voice Commands

When you can move away from your body, recall your initial intention, and use a word or phrase to call yourself into the experience you wished to have. I often use a simple word that connects to a feeling or movement, such that I can experience the effects of that word. These experiences, and thus your word choice, are personal for each of us. It's important not to focus on what others experience, or you will likely confuse yourself. Focus instead on your unique experience.

There are countless additional effects that you might experience during this phase. The essential things to remember right now:

1. Do not fear, no matter how strange or scary the experience may be.
2. Try to relax and let things play out naturally.
3. Try to move away from your body either by floating or by using thought.
4. Use voice commands to call yourself into the experience.

FURTHER REFLECTION

Now that you have had an out-of-body experience, you can wake up and reflect on what happened. If you were unsuccessful during the night, don't worry! You always have another night to try to achieve your goals. Often I will find that a few nights go by where nothing happens; if so, I work on relaxing more and learning from my previous experiences. Sometimes things are going on in my life that are stressful, and that is not the right time to have an out-of-body experience. It's a good idea to take care of any pressing matters before you start working on out-of-body experiences.

As with any practice, it's important to remember that failure is only one step closer to success. There is no such thing as truly failing; there is only learning. You can practice throughout the day by imagining yourself waking up from a dream and remembering what it was like, thinking about your daily intentions, or experimenting with the mindset that your thoughts and daily life are also dreamlike. Doing this regularly will bring you better lucidity during the night and help you continue to progress.

PART 3

•••

Working

with

Your Dreams

14

Awakening to the Potentials of Lucid Dreaming

Lucid dreaming comes with benefits and costs that may depend on your personal and cultural belief systems. Some believe that through lucid dreaming you can travel to other worlds or become enlightened, as Buddhist culture believes Siddhārtha Gautama did through his meditation practice. Other lucid dreamers take a more Western approach, finding value in communicating with the unconscious, removing mental blocks, and relieving ailments such as depression and PTSD. Still others believe that lucid dreaming, out-of-body experiences, and astral travel are harmful portals to the dark side.

Whatever your belief systems, there is a great deal of utility in lucid dreaming—but it also has its perils. Arming yourself with knowledge about the full spectrum of lucid dreaming's possible effects and outcomes can help you get the most out of your practice.

THE DANGERS OF LUCID DREAMING

In popular media, lucid dreaming is often portrayed in ways that are not possible, which has produced some of the concerns surrounding lucid dreams. In the movie *Inception,* for example, we see individuals hacking into others' minds and leaving false memories so that those individuals unwittingly change their habits. Although whether it's possible to share dreams is still an ongoing debate, changing or influencing someone's personal thoughts inside of a dream is definitely not possible. However, dying in a dream—another popular movie subject—and pursuing personal desires in dreams are encouraged as a healthy, safe way to process these experiences and sensations.

Experiencing or experimenting with trauma in a dream state has been shown to be an effective way to understand the process of life and death and the realization that fear and our natural responses to fear can be controlled in healthy ways. Personally, understanding fear and mortality in dreams have made a positive impact on how I react to fear-inducing experiences.

Dreams, however, can cause an individual to lose their grasp on reality if that individual's waking reality is not grounded in a holistic practice of psychological and spiritual awareness and healthy ego development. In other words: if someone focuses entirely on his or her dreams and uses them as an escape from real life, issues will arise. This doesn't make lucid dreaming in itself dangerous; it simply means that dreams are a means to understand reality more deeply—not a means to escape from it. Indulging in the latter will not lead to the true personal growth people are often seeking when they discover lucid dreaming in the first place.

NIGHTMARES AND FEARFUL EXPERIENCES

Any dream, lucid or not, can result in some pretty disconcerting experiences, as we have discussed earlier. We've all had nightmares that wake us, disoriented and spooked, with a pounding heart. When you start to consciously practice lucid dreaming, it is possible that you will become more aware of frightening dream experiences. If you are not ready for this, it can come as a shock. Worse, it can bring you face-to-face with troubling complexes and archetypes within the unconscious. Sleep paralysis, as well as hypnagogia, can create the sensation of not being able to move and induce troubling hallucinations in the process.

Additionally, false awakenings can cause some people to discontinue lucid dreaming. The idea of waking up over and over again while being stuck inside of a dream can be frustrating for some, but panic inducing for others. The best way to work through these experiences is to understand that you can't be hurt during a dream. Remember, these experiences are all quite common for lucid dreamers. You may even wish to take a break from lucid dreaming and talk about your experiences with someone you trust, such as a fellow lucid dreamer, therapist, or counselor.

ENLIGHTENMENT

The Tibetan Buddhist practice of dream yoga has one purpose: to end suffering. Many Buddhists believe that life is based on a cycle of death and rebirth and that in order to end this continuous cycle, one must understand the true nature of reality. Although it can take years of Buddhist study and practice to even begin to comprehend this, in Tibetan culture lucid dreaming is one tool to help move through the process.

In order to do this, it's important to realize that the dream world is made up of pure images produced by the unconscious, or what dream yoga practitioners call awareness. Once you realize that the dream world is an illusion, you can experience dreams of true awareness, or what the Tibetan practice calls a white light dream. These white light dreams ultimately lead to an understanding of reality and enlightenment. This approach to lucid dreaming can allow gifted lucid dreamers to have a more meaningful spiritual life through their experiences in the understanding of reality.

TRAVELING TO OTHER WORLDS

Many lucid dreamers firmly believe that lucid dreams take place in their own alternate reality. Once the dreamer travels through the portal of our conscious reality (a window or door in their house or place of sleep), they enter other worlds and experience real events in those realities. Some such dreamers say they have saved other worlds from destruction and taken part in Star Wars–like experiences across the universe.

One benefit of having these experiences is that the dreamer can enjoy a more adventurous life. However, we also see how they can produce problems. The degree of realism in some lucid dreams can cause some individuals to have trouble differentiating between our real world and their alternate world. If they bring personas, attitudes, or actions that would seem normal in a lucid dream into the reality we collectively know, it can have very real and sometimes long-lasting consequences.

TRADITIONAL USE OF LUCID DREAMS

If we look at history, we can see that there are ways that lucid dreaming has been used by societies to make long-lasting positive changes in the community.

Besides the Egyptians and Tibetans, dreams and lucid dreaming have been a large part of Native American cultures. In Lee Irwin's book *The Dream Seekers: Native American Visionary Traditions of the Great Plains,* we see that understanding big dreams was an important part of how indigenous cultures expressed their spirituality. We also know that shamanic traditions around the world have used dreams as essential ways of discovering their spiritual relationship to the world. Mircea Eliade's *Shamanism: Archaic Techniques of Ecstasy* is an exhaustive discussion of the traditional shamanic uses of dream awareness.

It seems that, in the past, dreams and lucid dreaming were a much larger part of many cultures than they are today in the Western world. In our current American culture we are encouraged to ignore our dreams as irrelevant, meaningless noise.

Rubin Naiman, of the Weil Center in Tucson, believes that cultures in which individuals integrate their dreams and lucid dreams into daily life not only have a greater understanding of their place in the community but also experience less depression and fewer cases of mental illness.

UNCONSCIOUS COMMUNICATION

The greatest benefit of lucid dreaming experiences is the ability to communicate with the mind in a more visual and unusual way. During a dream, you can conduct experiments to find out the limitations of the dream world and human consciousness. You can speak with your unconscious self or with the archetypes that contribute to the discovery of the true, integrated self. A personal relationship with the unconscious can be achieved through lucid dreaming (something that, incidentally, Sigmund Freud believed to be impossible).

THE DIFFERENCES BETWEEN DREAM EXPERIENCES

Because lucid dreams, out-of-body experiences, and astral projection can transform and merge into one another along a spectrum, it becomes difficult to draw hard lines between each experience. (Personally, I do not have a perfect definition for each of these states or for what state of consciousness I am in because I don't think it truly matters.) Often during a lucid dream an individual can feel the effects of an out-of-body experience by leaving the body while remaining in control of the environment. This is closer to a lucid dream state. Lucid dreams can also transform into astral projections, in which someone can experience the astral realm and travel to seemingly infinite dimensions.

Ultimately, the levels of waking and dream consciousness—the physical, the mental, and the astral—influence one another. We all experience all the levels of consciousness simultaneously, but our awareness stays locked into one level at a time. Lucid dreaming helps us practice shifting perspectives by loosening this locked-in style of paying attention. When we hold awareness in our dreams, we are manipulating the levels outside the dream at the same time. This gives our dreams tremendous power to influence our waking lives and also shows us that waking reality can greatly affect our dreams.

15

Guides and Guardians
of the Dream

ream characters can be as dynamic as the dreams themselves. Often, these dream characters can be broken into a few groups.

MINDLESS

This type of dream character seems to be preprogrammed to do particular tasks but when asked questions often has nothing to contribute to the dreamer. These characters are easily tricked and typically have little insight into the dream world, often having the sense that they believe they are not a product of a dream but are living and awake. Here are two examples of mindless dream characters from my own dreams:

Dream 1: I am at a college in Boise and notice that I am dreaming. Knowing I am lucid, I decide to go find people and ask them questions. I find a large church and go inside. Inside are a number of people all doing homework. I ask them what they are doing, and they reply, "Doing homework." They have no other answer and no description of the homework they are doing.

Dream 2: I become lucid in a building. I see several people around me and ask them if they want to see a magic trick. They say, "Sure." I say I could make a million dollars appear with the word abracadabra. *I say, "Abracadabra!" and then nothing happens. The dream characters express how lame the trick was, but I ask them to wait a moment. Soon enough a woman walks down the stairs with a suitcase, opens it, and inside is a million dollars. The dream characters ask how I did it, and I reply, "It's magic."*

INTELLIGENT

These insightful dream characters can answer complex questions that the dreamer may not know the answer to. They also know things that the dreamer may not know about the dream world or reality. For example:

I become fully lucid in a dream state. I go to my front door and walk through it. I meet an older woman who tells me her name is Jabooty (whom I later identify as a feminine aspect of my psyche). I ask her if I have known her before, and she says yes. I ask her what I should do with my life, and she says that what we should all do with our lives is quite simple: we should enjoy it and take care of it. She says she has to go because she is playing games with some kids.

Another dream of mine features a different manifestation of this kind of dream character:

I am at work and notice that my hair is standing on end as though I am under water, and then become aware that I am dreaming. I look around the building for a panda because I had intended to find a panda before I fell asleep. I find the panda, but it is a person with dark eyes and dark ears. I laugh at the idea, and he laughs, too. I ask him about the reality of dreams, and he tells me that dreams are real and not real at the same time. He says that dreams are a way for our subconscious mind to communicate with other people's subconscious and dreams are a visual representation of that. I find it interesting and continue on my dream.

GUARDIANS

The last type of lucid dream characters we'll discuss here are what I call guardians. Carl Jung would call these unconscious complexes—or archetypes, depending on the imagery experienced. Other dream experts, such as Ryan Hurd, call them visitors. These dream characters often offer strong emotional lessons to the dreamer and appear as monsters or as intense feelings—from dread to elation. They often present as independent dream characters during sleep paralysis, during a lucid dream that the dreamer is actively trying to control, or during out-of-body experiences. It is theorized that guardians can be generated by the individual psyche or by the universal collective consciousness, known as the objective psyche.

Interestingly, dreamers across cultures and identities report similar sensory experiences that signal a guardian. There does seem to be a universal quality to this type of dream character and the way the brain and psyche process it. Dreamers typically hear the sound of bells, screeching metal, or the shuffling of feet across the floor just before a guardian is seen.

Many common monsters appear in guardian encounters as well. Succubi, vampires, crones, witches, and warlocks all show up in our nightmares (a term, by the way, derived from the word *mære,* which means incubus, evil spirits believed to harm sleepers).

We have to ask: If these characters are often so scary, why call them guardians? As possible manifestations or projections of emotions we perceive as negative (and likely suppress), guardians show us a part of ourselves that we need to see. They are like reflections in a mirror trying to guide us in directions that will ultimately help us in our waking life. Often, when lucid dreamers accept these characters and their messages, they feel better about themselves and rarely have the same guardian encounter again.

What to Do If a Guardian Appears in a Dream

Keep in mind that the kind of healing and growth that can be accessed through guardians depends on a strong and prepared ego. If the ego of the lucid dreamer is not ready to consciously encounter archetypal imagery, it can do more harm than good. That is why it is important to practice lucid dreaming as part of a holistic approach that keeps us grounded and aware in waking life. Having a strong relationship with self-development also helps to process emotionally troubling dreams before continuing with further lucid dreaming.

> I notice a shadowlike figure in my room. I run at the figure to try to scare it or destroy it. After several attempts, the figure dissolves. I walk down the hall. I become aware that I want to face my fears and accept the shadowy figure. I think about seeing that guardian, and it appears. I am afraid, but I walk up to the character and ask what it wants. "I'm unsatisfied," it says. "Why? About what?" I ask. It says it doesn't know. I then see another guardian character walking toward us. We all sit down; I mold them into each other like clay, and they disappear.

Guardians appear in innumerable forms—they may be scary or aggressive—and what they do and ask of us in dreams is just as diverse; some guardians can present complex strategies or puzzles. However they behave and whatever they offer, the dreamer's role is to listen with an open heart. Try to identify the guardian's message, respond to the guardian in the dream, understand the consequences of acting on the guardian's message, and integrate that message into your life. Talking with a counselor or depth psychologist about guardian encounters can help in processing the complex messages that guardians sometimes bring.

16
Symbols
Keys to the Unconscious

Humans interact with the world through symbols. We use them to communicate, to define and study life, and to interact with our own minds. Symbols are not only the intentional cultural representations of concepts, such as language; they are also the meaning we imbue objects with. An owl can represent wisdom, winter may represent dormancy and death, red might mean danger or stop, green could mean go, and so on. Even characters—in fiction and in dreams—function on a symbolic level as they can personify qualities in the dream world and in ourselves, allowing us to describe something that is unconscious. We are able to navigate our communication and thoughts at lightning speed thanks to symbols.

You could make the argument that the dream world is all symbolic. When we are dreaming, the unconscious expresses its desires to us through symbols. Though we may not immediately understand what our dream imagery means to us, noticing it and thinking about why it holds personal meaning can open us up to lessons and wisdom from the unconscious, both collective and personal. Building a personal vocabulary of dream symbols can make our dreaming practice more fluent and rewarding.

Most of us have awakened from a dream and wondered, *What did it mean?* as if there were an external repository of dream symbol interpretations that were objectively true for everyone. And there is merit to the idea that many symbols operate on a macro level as widely accepted cultural tropes or memes, or as part of a collective unconscious. Falling, being chased, and teeth falling out are some of the more common dream images. Such images may or may not reflect parts of the collective psyche in the form of archetypal expressions. But in fact, there is no need for anyone to interpret what your dream means other than you. It is your own perspective on your dream images that helps you understand their meaning.

Jungian dream analysis is an excellent starting point for anyone who is trying to understand this process. Carl Jung himself interacted with his own dreams. He knew that every aspect of a dream, even something seemingly unimportant, is an expression of the psyche. His method of active imagination allows us to bridge our conscious and subconscious states and more actively (as the term suggests) engage in meaningful dialogue with our dreams.

Jung proposed that dream symbols are expressions of complexes and archetypes, universally defined human characteristics. Characters who present themselves in dreams often serve as archetypal expressions; their hair, eyes, clothing, personality, size, stature, language, and more may have symbolic meaning. By interacting with these symbols, we can affect how we experience the dream, alter the dream environment altogether, and, most importantly, acquire knowledge and understanding well past what we think is possible.

One key concept at the center of Jung's ideas and methods—a point that new oneirologists can easily lose sight of—is that we communicate with the unconscious through symbols. Without them, dream interpretation is a dead end. When we receive information from the unconscious through symbols, we can bring those symbols from the dreamscape into the 3D world. We can also communicate to the unconscious through understanding those symbols. This deep conversation is where the magic of lucid dreaming happens.

BRINGING DREAM SYMBOLS TO LIFE

One powerful way to work with dream symbols is to introduce them into your waking environment. An item from a dream that keeps you company during the day goes from being a fleeting image to being a presence in your life, giving you the physical time and space to contemplate it and for the symbol to work in your unconscious. I'll give you an example of how this works from my own practice.

> I once dreamed there was a panda in my room. Since I don't typically encounter pandas in my room, it felt significant, as if that panda— whatever it symbolized—had some reason to be there. So I made a clay panda and set it on my bedside table. A few days later, I had a lucid dream in which a man showed up. He had a dark patch around his eye, as if he'd been in a fight, and dark and light patches of hair. I asked, "Are you a panda?" He said he was, and I proceeded to ask him some questions about dreams and reality.

To do this for yourself, simply notice which symbols in your dreams feel significant. You don't need to be able to explain them right away— in fact, things that feel puzzling or intriguing, that inspire curiosity or just seem odd, may be ripe for the kind of slow unfolding that can happen with this practice.

The next step is to give the symbol a physical form. The options here are nearly endless, but here are some ideas:

- Write a word from your dream, using lettering and colors that feel relevant. Make it big and put it on a wall or the fridge, or make it small and carry it in your pocket.
- Draw or paint a picture, or take a photograph. Keep it by your bedside, or hang it on a wall.
- Make a representation of your dream image with clay, paper, or other material.

- Find a toy or model—a boat, a car, a spaceship, a doll—that resembles your dream symbol.
- Make use of ordinary objects that have been elevated to a place of significance by imitating their dream context. For example, if a pencil or coffee cup was floating in air in a dream, you might hang its real-world counterpart from a string or a hook.
- Collect objects you find in nature, such as rocks, leaves, or sand. Place them in a display case or place of honor in your bedroom.

Physical items don't necessarily have to be handmade, but there does seem to be something about the physical creative act that strengthens the symbol's connections between conscious and unconscious. Whatever you choose, the important thing is to raise your awareness that the symbol holds a part of you that has its own consciousness, and to invite that symbol to communicate with you.

You can also introduce symbols and concepts from the waking world that you want to explore in lucid dreams. The technique for this is similar to working with physical symbols that originate in dreams, but now the symbols come from the conscious, awake you. Some possibilities for generating symbols:

- If there's an idea you want to work with, distill it into one or two words, such as *creativity* or *purpose*. Recite it as a mantra, write it several times in a journal each day, or make it into a poster to meditate on.
- Find or create an image or object that symbolizes a significant event, idea, or feeling. Meditate on it, and invite your unconscious to help you discern its meaning for you.
- Decide that the sound of a bell in your dream will cue an important insight or feeling that you need. Select a bell (chime, bicycle ringer, or other instrument), and keep it in a designated place. Before starting your lucid dreaming practice each night, ring the bell.
- Follow your intuition. This may be the most important and most

effective technique. Simply notice what objects or images call to you, and then welcome them into your space, no matter how incongruous or random they may seem. When you prepare to lucid dream, ask the symbol to come with you into your dreams, and then ask your unconscious what it has to tell you about the symbol.

When you start meditating on a symbol—and simply introducing it to your reality is a way to meditate—you tell your unconscious to join in the dialogue about it. It may soon show up in a dream, where you can identify the symbol and draw out more information.

When creating your own lucid dreaming symbols, remember that a symbol doesn't need to be an object or image. It can be a word, a sound, a color—virtually anything can serve as a personal symbol as long as it has emotional meaning for you. Peer into your mind and memory, and find something valuable to you that you identify with and that you connect with the message you're trying to hear. Here's an example of a lucid experience I had after I'd been focusing on the words *higher self* for a while:

> I become aware that I'm dreaming, and in my dream I yell, "Higher self!" I find myself on the moon. On the moon, there is a mirror, and I look at myself. The message feels clear to me. I become aware that my "higher self" is simply myself; I just have to look within.

FAKE IT TILL YOU MAKE IT

Lucid dreaming is, at its heart, a practice of the imagination. It puts us in direct contact with the heady idea that our dreams are as real as waking life, and that waking life is as much a product of imagination as our dreams are. So in order for the whole practice to work, you have to believe the symbols will work. If doubt is proving to be a stumbling block in your work with dream symbols, there are a few ways to get around it.

First and probably most important is to feel a real connection to whatever symbol you decide to work with. This applies no matter how personal or mundane the symbol is. There are plenty of esoteric symbols only an internet search away that look cool or have amazing stories attached to them. But will they work for you? Considering Jung's observation of the collective unconscious character of some symbols, along with his theory of synchronicity, a glyph you find in a seemingly random search may indeed have something to teach you. But it is not something you need to give much weight to. A symbol doesn't need to be esoteric, impress anyone else, or come at the end of an exhaustive search; it just needs to be vital for you.

One example of a universal symbol that also has profound personal meaning for me is the Ouroboros, a symbol I experienced in the middle of a dream:

> . . . and as I lie on the ground, a large creature slides up to me. It opens its mouth, and I recognize that it's a giant snake. It swallows me whole, and as I go down its throat, the same snake appears and eats me again and again . . .

This dream is laden with meaning. It speaks to the repetitive nature of life, to the possible futility of the continuous search for self-knowledge, and—salient for me personally—the danger of slipping into stagnancy and complacency if I continue to do the same things over and over again.

Symbols are the vocabulary, the grammar, and the language of dreams. When you commit to a lucid dreaming practice, you also commit to learning your mind's own symbolic language. As you call up more and more symbols for examination, you will increase your facility in navigating your own dreams, improve your meditation practice, and likely begin to have out-of-body experiences. So starting today, make your own symbols. It will introduce you to levels of inner wisdom and strength that you weren't aware of before.

17

Dream Interpretation

History and Practice

For every person who has wondered what their dreams mean, there is another person ready and willing to give an answer. Many people on the internet today—from well-meaning aficionados to purported experts to outright snake-oil salesmen—swear they can interpret others' dreams for them. There are even automated systems that can analyze a dream's symbology or text and spit out a message for the dreamer. In every instance, an attempt to interpret someone else's dream, especially that of a stranger, and without context, is a waste of time and money at best and interferes with the dreamer's development at worst. Dream content is unique to each dreamer in specific ways that are not intended for outsiders to access or understand in the way the dreamer should.

MODERN DREAM INTERPRETATION: A SHORT HISTORY

Psychologists have been attracted to dreaming as a portal into human consciousness since the profession was born over a century ago. It's important to remember that dream studies did not begin with modern psychology—references to dreams as sources of prophecy, healing, and intra- and trans-personal communication date all the way back to ancient Greek and Judeo-Christian texts. However, the past hundred years have brought dream interpretation into the widespread consciousness for better and for worse.

Most of the popular modern dream interpretation today—the dream dictionaries and auto-interpreters available online, for example—stems from the work of Sigmund Freud. He believed that common symbology in a dream can be traced back to the basic human evolutionary impulses for sex, violence, and greed. Though many psychologists and oneirologists now strongly disagree with Freud, he was also right in some important foundational ways. Mainly, he reminded a modern, industrialized world that dreams can point us toward meanings that conscious experience alone cannot provide. Freud also proved to have a huge influence on the general public's appreciation of dreams and dream studies.

Carl Jung, who was at one time a student of Freud, ultimately parted ways with his teacher's philosophies to become possibly the most important pioneer of modern dream interpretation. His models of two-way communication between dreamer and analyst, as well as his ideas about the role of archetypes and the collective unconscious in individuals' dreams, are still used today. Jung's way of looking at dreams allowed for the much-needed personal insight that comes when we interpret our own dreams. He also viewed dreams as being a message about today or the future, not about the past. Many people still use Jung's method of dream interpretation, and others have built onto his processes. One example of this is Medard Boss and his development of existential psychoanalysis of dreams.

Unlike Freud and Jung, Medard Boss, a Swiss psychoanalyst who was mentored by German existential philosopher Martin Heidegger, viewed a dream as a human experience with its own value rather than as simply a symbol trying to convey hidden information. According to Boss, a dream experience is sufficient in itself: it doesn't need to be dissected, just understood. Although at first this stance may seem a bit disappointing to the avid lucid dreamer, it may actually be a valuable method for consistently remembering dreams. Simply documenting dreams as they arise can help the dreamer with reality checks and in developing a personal symbology visible to the conscious mind—actions that can do their own unconscious work on the dreamer.

Among modern dream scholars, Ann Faraday may be one of the most influential and revered. Her 1990 book, *The Dream Game,* offers an interpretation technique much like Boss's approach and is also one of the best techniques I've found. In a dialogue, the analyst guides the dreamer (in a clinical setting) to recall their dreams in whatever form or order they arise in their conscious memory. Subsequent conversation leads the dreamer to interpret the dream for themselves and to recall further details. This process of essentially transforming a dream into a narrative provides the dreamer with their own story from which to derive meaning.

THE TAO OF
DREAM INTERPRETATION

Is there a right way to interpret dreams? Is there a set of best practices that help guarantee success? Is it necessary to try (or even learn about) all of the countless methods? The answer to all of these questions is no. Interpreting dreams can be like any spiritual practice; such a practice is built one step at a time with equal parts tradition and direct personal experience. Like the Chinese concept of the Tao, interpreting dreams is best achieved by interacting with the yin and yang of our spirit via a middle way—open to wonder and insight, yet focused sincerely on the daily practices that get you there. That said, there are a few interpretation practices that I have found produce consistently excellent results.

First, the basic understanding of dream psychology and physiology that we've been establishing will support you enormously; it will ground you in your sensory, perceptual, and physical self as you explore the dream self.

Next, we can take a lesson from Ann Faraday and practice dream recall: first writing down and then recounting vocally every possible detail from the dream, and then repeating the dream from the beginning until it feels like a story from which we can derive some meaning. Last, recall how specific points in the dream and its content affect you emotionally. Look at the direct, overt, or more universal nature of the symbols and their emotional context in your own life. Dreams do not refer to the past—they convey messages relevant today—so the dream symbols and content should be relevant to what is currently happening or to what may be happening soon.

I like to think of the dream as a friend trying to tell me something: sometimes it's a bit cryptic, but there is always a message. So listen as you would listen to a friend, and stay open and patient. Once I feel I understand what a dream is saying, I can choose to accept the message or deny it. Accepting the dream and its message may be all that is needed to interpret your own dream.

These practices provide a solid foundation as long as you remember the most important principles of dream interpretation:

Your dreams are unique.

Others' dreams are unique to them.

The best person to understand a dream is the dreamer. Being honest with yourself and willing to listen to what a dream has to say is key to dream interpretation.

DREAMS ARE MULTILAYERED

Dreams can have multiple layers of meaning and can express their intended messages through a symbolic representation that applies both psychologically and physically. These messages can be hard to understand at times because you may find one meaning that makes sense to you, and that you identify as the underlying story of what needs to be addressed in your life, while missing entirely another element that is expressing itself in your personal actions.

A good example is in a dream I had that included visiting the underworld:

I find myself in my room. There, I meet a woman who radiates gold as an essence of her being, and I find that it is important to follow her. As we pass into the dream world through my bedroom window, she leads me through a veil of the living and the dead. As I pass through the veil, I find myself surrounded by what seem to be dead people. They notice me and start to come closer. I look for the woman of gold, and she is nowhere to be found. The undead beings start to drain out my essence of life just by touching me. I become frightened and run away just in the nick of time.

After waking from this dream, I found myself later that day struck with a depressed mood and fatigue that I had not experienced before. I ignored the dream and my reaction and, as weeks and months passed by, I found myself becoming more exhausted. After finally consulting a doctor, I found that a parasite was active in my body and was physically draining my energy. After identifying this cause, I thought that surely the dream was about the parasite and took the treatment that the doctor recommended, but my energy level still continued to plummet.

I was soon referred to a psychologist as the doctor had run out of reasons for my continued illness. The psychologist discussed my activities during the day and the many projects I had going on. It wasn't until after identifying that the many projects in my life were also acting as parasites on my mental energy that I began to heal.

This was an important lesson for me to learn about understanding dreams. Dreams can be extremely complex and their messages encoded. The initial assumption of the dream and its meaning may be correct, but the prescription may be multifaceted. As in my case, the issue resided in my psychical and mental activity, both of which had to be addressed before I could start to heal.

Dream Interpretation Cheat Sheet

All you need to know to start interpreting your dreams. Practice consistently and observe how your dreams unfold for you.

1. Sit comfortably, and close your eyes. Remember the dream from beginning to end. Recall every detail you can: smells, colors, textures, sounds, tastes, people and other characters, surroundings, temperature, thoughts, conversation, emotion. . . .

2. Recall the dream again *as if for the first time*. Do this as many times as you feel is necessary.

3. Listen to any internal voices or intuitions you have about what the dream has to say.

4. Consider how the story is meaningful to you personally. Often, the first meaning you sense is the right one.

If you engage with this process for a while and still feel stuck, you might consider sharing the dream with a trusted friend or counselor. Someone with more experience in this method may be able to help you find ways to recall more details or see the story from a different angle—without directly offering their own interpretations—that will unlock meaning for you. Anyone with a strong foundation in dream psychology can be a helpful and trustworthy dream guide.

If you still find yourself stuck, don't worry. Set the dream aside for a while—it may have information you'll be more ready to hear later. Or try lucid dreaming for more direct exploration.

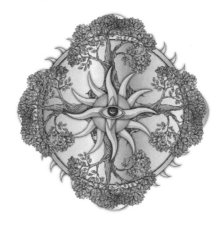

18
Dream Companions
Mentors, Guides, Friends

So far we've seen that lucid dreaming is a deeply personal practice and that dream interpretation is a highly individualized art. And yet dreaming is universal. It's only human to want to share our dream experiences. How do we connect with others without interfering in the delicate conversation between the conscious and unconscious mind? We can find support and community in trusted friends and mentors, books, and, somewhat recursively, the guides in our own dreams.

MENTORS

Talking with others about dreams can strengthen dream recall and the desire to have more dreams, but with the wrong person it can be disheartening. Early on in my dream practice, I didn't fully trust the value of dreams myself, and I shared dreams with people who dismissed their value. But as I started to think critically, dive into the symbology of my dreams, and see them as more than just random noise that happens when we sleep, I found a mentor who could understand and wanted to listen. Soon my insights and memory improved. The detached perspective of an interested but neutral listener accelerated my learning and opened my mind to new interpretive possibilities. I stopped listening to the naysayers and took the steps to make up my own mind.

Mentors don't always offer direct assistance. Another mentor of mine was a roommate who, it turned out, suffered from schizophrenia. He experienced hallucinations of snakes and other troubling images. He explained that he had come to accept these figures as part of his reality and that he no longer feared them. I took his wisdom to heart and tried to accept the frightening images in my dreams as a startling but ultimately nonthreatening aspect of myself that was desperately trying to convey a message.

Mentors can also lead us astray. Some people I have encountered have given me information that was inaccurate, didn't apply to my experiences, or left no room for my personal experience. I found their rigid "tell it like it is" approach to be imprisoning to my creative mind. Rather than let them limit my experiences, I took their advice with a grain of salt and moved on to others who had personally experienced things I was talking about and who knew how to guide me.

BOOKS AND ONLINE RESOURCES

There is something powerful about reading. It allows us to take time to absorb and explore new ideas deeply and then reflect on them. Another amazing thing about a book is that you never know when the right book will walk into your life at the perfect time.

When I was accepted into a military flight program, a friend of mine gifted me a book, *Mozart's Brain and the Fighter Pilot,* by Richard Restak, M.D. This friend gave it to me because of *fighter pilot* in the title, but the book wasn't about flying fighter jets at all. It was about self-improvement through logic and objective reasoning, not the kind of thing I was into at the time. However, since it was a gift, I gave it a try. This book ended up blowing my mind, and reading it became a decisive moment in my quest into lucid dreaming.

I am not saying that everyone should go out and purchase that book (although I do think it's useful and fascinating). I share the anecdote to show how the ideas that have the power to initiate a journey of self-discovery will often appear synchronically in forms and at times that you wouldn't seek out yourself. They are clues to your inner journey. When events like this happen, they're opportunities to follow those clues and take in the new ideas they're offering.

Ready for a deeper dive into interpreting your dreams? These resources delve into the history of dream studies, explore the latest dream science, and offer guidance for developing your own dream practice and for interpreting personal dream symbols.

An Introduction to the Psychology of Dreaming, by Kelly Bulkeley, Ph.D.—This comprehensive survey covers developments in dream research and interpretation over the past one hundred years, from Freud and Jung to the latest neuroscience and brain imaging studies. Each chapter discusses a different aspect of the science of dreams, all seeking answers to the guiding questions: How do we dream? What are dreams for? What can we do with them?

The Dream Game, by Ann Faraday—Faraday's classic guidebook for remembering, interpreting, and learning from dreams takes you step-by-step through establishing a dream journal, tracking dreams, and working with the messages your dreams have for you.

Inner Work, by Robert A. Johnson—A helpful guide to understanding dreams through depth psychology. Johnson provides an easy-to-understand process for diving deeply into each dream, pulling out the relevant information, and using active imagination to open and strengthen the lines of communication with your unconscious.

Dream Studies Portal, dreamstudies.org—Trained in archaeology, consciousness studies, and dream studies, the oneirologist, author, and educator Ryan Hurd maintains the Dream Studies Portal as a place for readers to investigate dream research, consciousness, and their own dream images and practice.

My website, "taileaters.com/discussion," is a place to get involved with others interested in this topic.

DREAM GUIDES

Dream characters can also act as powerful mentors. They can hold important information about our dreams, and that information can then bleed into waking life. Remember the panda that appeared in my dream? I decided to find out if he was a dream guide who would interact with me further. Sure enough, after I set that intention he started appearing in my dreams. In one lucid dream I walked up to him.

> *"Are dreams real?" I ask.*
> *"Yes and no," he says. "Dreams are the space in between reality, where others' unconsciousness can meet and interact with each other in a version of reality."*

I found this message to be profound and validating, and it allowed me to explore Jung's ideas about the collective unconscious as a possible reality and not just a theoretical concept.

In addition to granting insights from dream characters, dreams themselves can offer the gift of insight into the internal struggles that we are aware of. These dreams provide guidance around the under-standing that we are more than just our consciousness.

> *I'm walking on the moon again. A young boy is digging holes in the ground, just as I did when I was young. There is something odd about him—shy and in his own world, like I was as a kid. He asks me to join him; I tell him I will think about it, and then I don't join him. He has seen through my lie and is upset. He jumps into one of the holes. Jabooty (a female representation of my psyche who has appeared in other dreams) appears again and tells me that she would deal with the little boy. "He's always acted this way. It's no big deal!" she says.*

Dream guides also can transform over time. What was once a panda might evaporate in another dream into a sense or feeling or even a wind that pulls the dreamer in a particular direction. In the stories of myth, heroes are often launched into their journey not by a physical being but by a feeling or calling that captures their attention. Dream guides can act the same way.

FRIENDS

The most important dream guides and mentors are our friends. Friends play huge roles in our lives and in how we see ourselves. The people we attract into our lives are mirrors that show us parts of ourselves that are difficult to see, or that are invisible to ourselves. As such, they have much to teach us.

If you've had a long-term friendship or intimate relationship, then you know that those people change over time just like we do and our complexes that make up our personalities do. The reality of their lives and our lives, along with our perceptions of ourselves and of each other, form a kaleidoscope of recognition. We are painting a picture that's constantly changing. No one version is the real or final version, but each iteration has something new to tell us if we are willing to listen. Investigating those new angles and versions to understand aspects of the self can guide us toward understanding who we are and reaching who we want to be.

DREAM INTERPRETATION GROUPS

Craig Chalquist, Ph.D., who teaches and writes about personal and collective transformation at the Worldrede website, provides some useful techniques for bringing out the meaning of a dream in group work. His twelvefold dream solution is based on principles of depth psychology with a bit of an alchemical twist. It comprises what Chalquist calls a "reexperiencing phase," in which the dreamers use storytelling techniques to recount and begin to examine symbols in their dreams, followed by a meaning-making phase, which entails viewing the dream through various lenses and contexts to extract potential meanings. Here is a summary of the process:

REEXPERIENCING PHASE:

1. **Containing:** All listeners agree to keep the dream in the room and to be courteous in their comments about the dream.
2. **Telling:** Tell the dream once through in the present tense. Bring listeners into the dream, and be inside it as you speak.
3. **Setting:** Go into the details of the dream's very beginning. This provides the context for the situation commented on by the dream.
4. **Decoding:** Open up the symbols with free associations to each and by evoking the details of each. Do dream characters seem exactly like people or not?
5. **Embodying:** Sit for a moment with the images, sensations, and emotions brought up. Where is the dream in your body? What senses does it involve?
6. **Reflecting:** Focus on the dream ego. Where is it in the dream? How do its behavior and reactions parallel how it behaves and reacts during the day?
7. **Conversing:** Engage key figures in lengthier active imaginations. Invite them into the room. Ask them to respond to the dream ego.

MEANING-MAKING PHASE:

8. **Distilling:** Gather up the dream as a whole. What is it saying?
9. **Multiplying:** What does it say on personal, cultural, archetypal, ecological, chronological, and spiritual levels?
10. **Projecting:** Where else outside of you does the dream show up? How do its motifs play out in your relationships, in class, at work, locally, or in the culture at large?

11. **Tincturing:** What title would you give this dream? Does it want next steps? Does it want to be expressed creatively through visuals, movement, or other forms? What place does it hold in a dream series, if any?

12. **Circulating:** These steps can be repeated more than once for the same dream, like refining the philosopher's stone by running it through the Magnum Opus again and again.

As the dreamer, you may be able to use Chalquist's process not only to better understand your own dreams but also to inspire yourself to have more vivid and impactful dreams in the future.

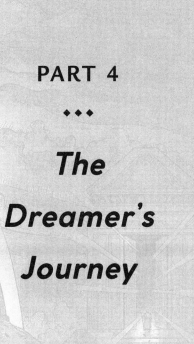

PART 4

•••

The Dreamer's Journey

19
The Shadow
Facing the
Dream's Darker Guides

Not all mentors are friendly. A good teacher—one who is firm and fair, who knows how to get through even to hard-headed and stubborn students like me—knows that sometimes the most direct route to the student's understanding is through fear. A teacher who gets in our face and pushes us toward the next steps they know we're ready for but are afraid to face can be exactly the inspiration we need. We can see nightmares and scary dream characters as just such tough-love mentors. They serve as our teachers and also as mirrors to those parts of ourselves that we'd rather not see.

Through imagery and our actions, we can find internal understanding and improve our reactions to fear and death. I myself have had plenty of nightmarish dreams that I've been able to turn into learning opportunities.

A monster made of glass comes out of the sink in my apartment. Its hands are contorted. I touch it and try to break off parts of it before it can come out, but I cannot stop it. I start to run away.

My roommate is in a different area of the house and yells to me about the monster trying to get him. He says the Watcher Man wants to get him but can't; he runs off and manages to get out of the apartment. The apartment starts to flood with water, and I worry about my belongings. I decide to go back into the apartment even though the monster is around. As I get to my room, the door at the end of the hallway breaks down. There stands a man made of glass and electricity. He grabs me, and I shatter into glass shards. I see others continue to run from him; some get away, and others don't. As he grabs people, I can see their souls leave their bodies and fade away. Music plays in the background.

This dream is filled with imagery that is both terrifying and insightful. The concept of life after death, as well as my experiencing my death in the dream, allowed me to face some of my deeper fears in life.

In the esoteric teachings of theosophists and philosophers such as Madame Blavatsky and Rudolf Steiner, when an individual is ready to start their journey into the deeper realms of spirit and mind, they are approached by a mentor known as the Guardian of the Threshold. This frightful, menacing being—monster, ghost, human, or other product of the imagination—represents a challenge, often an aspect of the individual's suffering, that must be surmounted before leveling up to the next stage. This concept of the Guardian accurately depicts what Jung described as the shadow. What better teacher than a manifestation of what that person sees as the worst inside themselves? The prospect of facing the shadow can be intimidating, but it's essential to self-awareness and growth, and dream work is one of the most powerful ways to achieve this.

The Guardian of the Threshold is often described in abstract terms, but dreaming is a chance to manifest the symbolic and near-physical. And the experience can feel all too real.

I awake to a conversation downstairs. I recognize the voices of my housemates, as well as my friend who is currently on deployment in Iraq. As soon as I realize it would be impossible for him to be home, the conversation stops. At this moment I see-sense a glowing blue orb floating up the stairs toward me.

Encounters with the Guardian of the Threshold in the form of a glowing orb of light is described frequently in dream accounts. Though to the outside listener it may sound benign, it can feel quite terrifying. Remember that, according to Jung, while many dream images and experiences are universal, the concepts we associate with them and our emotional reactions to them can be subjective and personal.

When you become aware of any emotion in a dream, the key is to notice it rather than to be seized by it. This is admittedly challenging when confronting a shadow figure. However, by using lucid dreaming techniques, you can become aware in your dream and thus detach yourself from any truly frightening action that takes place. The shadow is not something to judge or to disregard, but to accept and to merge with, as Jung writes. This process can also teach us how often we create our own suffering through our actions. Once you accept that, you are no longer restrained by assumptions, reactions, and inherited biases and beliefs.

Self-acceptance of disowned parts lies at the heart of shadow dream work. In his book *Journeys Out of the Body,* Robert Monroe writes that his astral body was breathing into his ear while his consciousness was split in two. He was frightened at first but later realized it was he who was scaring himself. This is a perfect articulation of facing the shadow. Jung references *The Strange Case of Dr. Jekyll and Mr. Hyde* to make the same point. "It must be Jekyll, the conscious personality, who integrates the shadow . . . and not vice versa. Otherwise the conscious becomes the slave of the autonomous shadow."

Further, Jung says, "ego and shadow are no longer divided but are brought together in an—admittedly precarious—unity."

According to Jung, the shadow presents itself organically; it makes itself known when the unconscious is ready for it to be seen. When this happens, it's up to the individual to allow him- or herself to see, and then understand or absorb, the shadow:

"[If] the life-mass is to be transformed . . . we have to expose ourselves to the animal impulse of the unconscious without identify-

ing with it and without "running away"; for flight from the unconscious would defeat the purpose of the whole proceeding. We must
hold our ground, which means here that the process initiated by
the dreamer's self-observation must be experienced in all its rami-
fications and then articulated with consciousness to the best of his
understanding."

Just as the corpus callosum bridges the left and right hemispheres
of the brain, and just as many individuals report a strong sense of unity
after a psychedelic experience, shadow work merges conscious and
unconscious parts of the personality. All these experiences are a meeting
of the minds, if you will. It could be, therefore, that the shadow integration we achieve through dreaming has a biochemical effect thanks
to changes in the brain's Default Mode Network. What follows is an
integration experience from one of my own dreams:

*I lie in bed expecting to face whatever was causing the experience to
happen. I want to move on. I go to sleep, and once again I can't move.
I look toward the doorway and see it open slightly. A being enters,
wearing a long robe and a hood covering its face. I get up and run,
frightened. I grab the being's cloak and eat it; it's screaming, and
the next thing I know I have devoured the entire being. The room
goes silent.*

Here the conscious self literally absorbs the shadow self, a merging
that is necessary to move forward on the journey. But there is another
layer to this shadow, and that is death itself. The dreamer faces the fear
of death. The being's menacing presence is overcome at the moment
when a sense of power outweighs the sense of fear. Rather than run
away or turn toward something or someone else for help, the dreamer
takes matters into his own hands. This marks a huge turning point,
because a person entering the psychospiritual world without having
encountered the Guardian of the Threshold can fall prey to one delu-
sion after another. He would never be able to distinguish between that

which he himself brings into that world and what actually belongs to it. But with repeated encounters, the dreamer becomes less frightened of the experience and more accepting of the task at hand. Eventually, the dreamer can even calm the masculine nature of the fight or flight response and explore solutions to these encounters through a more feminine response of trust and love, as shown in the following dream:

> *I'm talking with some people about the nature of dreams. They seem as confused as I am. I look around and, in a store, see a book with the panda on it. I recognize the panda is important, and suddenly the book is in my hand. I start turning the pages. I make out a face on the pages, and it changes slightly every time I turn the page, like a flipbook. As it animates I see it's a woman talking. The pages start to turn on their own, and I become scared. Suddenly there is silence, and a terrible dread fills me.*
>
> *Something is behind me. I turn around, and there's a girl. Her hair is black and falls over her face. I want to run but remember my first experience with the Guardian of the Threshold. I fly into the girl, as if diving into a pool of water.*

Later I learned to respect and love the shadow for what it is: all the fear, anger, and dissatisfaction that I meet life with. These feelings are not the life-giving, animated, youthful images my dreams were offering me; instead I experienced those qualities as threatening. The answer from my unconscious was, unsurprisingly, to up the ante and show me the emotions I was actually living. In my next dream, these emotions would appear in the form of zombies.

A zombie is a perfect representation of the half-lived lives many of us lead. They come complete with an unquenchable hunger for life in the form of human flesh (it's no wonder the zombie is such a key figure in horror movies and popular culture). In the dream below, a zombie represents both the archetype of the shadow and the theme of dissatisfaction that recurs in my own dream lexicon:

I walk out of my room and down a hallway. As I get to the kitchen I sense a presence and turn around. I know it's the shadow because I feel the same dread I always do. Rather than run away from it or attack it, this time I walk over to it. It looks like a zombie, and I know it's hungry for my brain. I bow my head and let it eat me. I feel the chomp of its mouth as it bites into my flesh. Then there's a calm. I look up (even though I've been eaten) and notice that it has stopped attacking. I ask it to sit down with me and talk. It does, and now I'm looking at a copy of myself.

I ask the copy what it wants from me. "I am unsatisfied," it says. I ask it what it's unsatisfied about, and it says it's just unsatisfied. Another zombie appears down the hallway, so I ask it to come sit with us. It sits down and turns into another copy of myself. They pull out wires from inside themselves, connect their wires together, and then merge into each other and then into me. I wake up.*

Though not all dream guides are supernatural and in symbolic form, we can still learn from them and use the tools they provide us to make progress on our journey. For what is described next, we will need all the help we can get.

---

*This dream is similar to a dream I discussed earlier (p. 86), but in that dream they were clay rather than wires.

20
The Call to Adventure

ike many of the heroes in iconic stories, who take amazing journeys and face unimaginable foes, average people can also be called to adventure. The adventure itself is not always as apparent or literal as it is in myth, fiction, or drama; it may in fact be hidden from our consciousness entirely. But whatever the adventure is, it will most definitely be as challenging and dramatically transformational as the heroic journeys that permeate our culture.

Joseph Campbell explained in his seminal analysis of the world's mythologies that average people are called to adventure, but responding to that call is optional. When the call is refused, an individual's life might appear to go on as usual, but—as Jung observed—the unconscious is at work, creating synchronicities and dreams that allow their destined adventure to take place internally, where opposing forces battle.

That's how the call to adventure played out for me, so I can attest that it can be an arduous process. It took me years of reflection to identify my adventure and to start to take steps toward integrating this journey into my life. It all started one fateful night in the late summer of 1997, when I was a normal thirteen-year-old growing up in the ordinary town of Meridian, Idaho.

I'm lying outside with a friend. We had been spending the summer sleeping under the stars. I see a bright light coming toward us. An airplane? No . . . it starts coming closer to us, then stops suddenly, then shoots straight up into the air and curves over the horizon and out of sight. We're both alarmed and stunned.

Not unlike the dream of the blue orb I would have fifteen years later, this felt like an otherworldly intrusion into my ordinary world. It was like a beacon pulling me toward a new direction. "Follow me; come see what else is in store," it seemed to say. But as a naive kid in a conventional environment, it was more intimidating than enticing. So I ignored it, removing it from my conscious thought.

In the intervening years, I continued to deny my call to the adventure of exploring worldviews that ran counter to my monotheistic upbringing. I became more depressed as my ego and my soul fought for control over my view of reality. It wasn't until after intense processing, reflection, and dream work that I accepted new beliefs and ways of thinking and was finally relieved of the chronic depression that had plagued me. It was as if a guardian had been haunting me, and then became integrated only when I fully confronted it. This integration is not a one-time fix. Facing the shadow is an ongoing process that will occur over and over again throughout our lives.

I declined my invitation to the Hero's Journey many times, but that doesn't mean I wasn't already on the journey. This sort of rejection is normal, as often we are not in the right place or the right state of mind to continue forward intentionally. The Hero's Journey is life itself, and every experience has something to teach us. If you don't know where your journey is taking you, or you're not even sure you want to be on a journey, don't be discouraged. The journey is inevitable. You are making progress. The sooner you recognize that and learn how to work with rather than against the synchronicities, symbols, and dreams all around you, the faster and further you can progress on your journey. The challenge, should you accept it, is to confront the Guardian of the Threshold and cross into the portal.

DOORWAYS
INTO THE DEPTHS

With a descent into the psyche, the individual must face the Guardian of the Threshold—that part of us that, according to Steiner's *An Outline of Occult Science,* stands at "the portals of physical death." When we overcome the Guardian of the Threshold, we answer the call to adventure and open the doorway to the Hero's Journey. These doorways—or portals, as they are commonly known in oneirology—appear in dreams in many forms: doors, windows, paintings, mirrors, holes—anything the imagination can conjure as a gateway to a new reality. Like Alice through the looking glass, we can use our dreams to step into a new adventure and new inner worlds.

> *I wake up in my room. The Grim Reaper—a cloaked figure, face shrouded—is coming for me, summoning me. I'm terrified, and then step back from my fear to observe it. I walk up to the figure, and in one swift motion, I eat him. I am alone in a vacuum of silence.*

A light shines from the hallway leading downstairs. As I cross through the doorway into the hall, I am suddenly walking down steps into a 1940s-style hotel lobby. Everything looks and feels real: granite walls, brass railing, the feeling of walking down the steps. I stop at a water fountain, cup my hand to drink from the fountain, and watch and feel the water moving over my hand. At the bottom of the stairs I walk into a dining area filled with people. They all stop and stare at me. I feel very out of place, and I know that this world would continue whether I'm here or not.

We may have many such dreams, as I have, in which we confront the Guardian of the Threshold and enter a new world. When those dreams leave us feeling as if we've achieved a new level of understanding, it can be thrilling: Who can I share this with? Or cause for concern: Am I crazy? If I tell anyone, will they think I'm crazy? The thoughts and judgments of others do not matter. These dreams and experiences don't need external validation; they're there for you alone. Talking to others may provide some guidance or encouragement, but there is enough in the dreams themselves to work with. From this point, you can embark on the adventure of exploring the nature of your dream world.

21
World Building in the Liminal Space

With consistent practice I've had amazing lucid dreams that verge on out-of-body experiences. Here, I can explore different worlds, time lines, and places that feel real but that are at best a kind of computer simulation created by my mind. More important than pondering the nature of these experiences, or simply enjoying the ride, it's vital to consider the weight of these dreams and what they can teach us.

To get the most out of lucid dreaming, perfect practice is paramount. To see how lucid dreaming techniques inform the dream experiences themselves, it helps to look at the anatomy of an actual dream. Notice especially the way reality checks are woven into this dream narrative:

I peer into a coat closet and feel a cold breeze coming through it. As I begin to walk inside, I feel dizzy and float the rest of the way in. I know that I am dreaming and open my eyes, but close them after seeing a very bright light. I try to speed up time, but instead it slows down. I go with it, try to slow down time even more, and time accelerates. This feels unsettling to me. I wake up to start writing down my dream, then realize I'm still dreaming.

I wake up, my body buzzing with energy. I tell myself, Open your eyes, *and find myself floating out of my body. I look around the room and see my wife and the cat are there. I ask my wife if she can see me; she says yes. As I move around the room, it is illuminated with a blue glowing light that is coming from within me.*

By checking externals for validation, you can be aware that you're dreaming, regardless of how anyone else in the dream (in this case, my wife) experiences it (talking with her about it later, she had no memory of answering me). The act of doing the check kicked off a dream experience that had a real effect. Accepting the dream's importance is what matters, not how real it is.

A clue that this dream sequence might have something important to say is that it begins with a portal. As soon as I walk into the coat rack, I feel transported, and by playing with controlling time and failing, I feel a strong warning not to believe too wholeheartedly in my ability to have conscious control of reality in this dream world or in the waking one.

That awareness—that you are dreaming and so have some control over your actions and over the trajectory of the dream, and yet at the same time have to surrender to the laws of a new world—is where the learning resides. The dream world is created by an awareness outside of your own conscious awareness, often described as the dream narrator. In a sense, you're a video game character who knows you're in a video game: you can control some aspects of the dream, but the narrator is always creating the world a step ahead of you.

Which opens up the question: If the dream narrator controls the dream, does it also control your level of lucidity? Sometimes lucidity is introduced by characters or objects in a dream, and it's our willingness to go with it—just like going with the laws of time in the previous dream—that wakes us up to the dream world. Much like how giving up control in our own lives can be a path to happiness, it is when we're willing to relinquish some control over our dream narratives that we become open to the wisdom of the unconscious.

I'm in a long line of students waiting to speak to the professor. I stand and wait; I talk with some other students. . . . I'm called up and sit down. "What seems to be the problem?" the professor asks. He takes my arm and points out a black spot on my arm. "That's the source of your troubles," he indicates. He tells me he could fix me up right away and sticks a metal needle into my arm; immediately I become lucid. I decide to trust the professor and feel a rush of air blow over me. At once I'm floating over my bed.

By this point you may have been practicing lucid dreaming techniques and acquired some skill in exploring and manipulating your dreams. And now I'm suggesting that exercising control over your dream environments is bad? Not at all. Though Jung may say that trying to control the unconscious is treacherous, I believe that in expressing control we are, in a deeper sense, expressing the intent to communicate and understand. We are not manipulating the dreamscape—we are exploring it and responding as it unfolds. This is a delicate and exciting process. The excitement that comes from exploring dreams actively is a powerful catalyst toward individuation for many oneironauts. Additionally, active lucid dreaming satisfies the ego's drive to make astonishing discoveries and be "enlightened," so we can prove the value of the practice to others. This particular ego gratification is hard to bypass in our culture. And if it does lead to genuine discoveries, which it is proven to do, then it's a valid way to start exploring dreams. I don't look down on those who are aspiring to learn more about themselves through controlling their dreams.

Whatever our approach to exploring our dreams, making ourselves vulnerable to our unconscious parts and to cross over into the dream world takes enormous courage. We can't fully understand the dangers that await as we delve into the unconscious, but only in doing so can we discover the gem of our true selves.

22

Into Dangerous Waters

You've crossed the portal and explored or built a new world. You've agreed (or at least relented) to embarking on your Hero's Journey. Now we wade into waters that feel truly dangerous.

Joseph Campbell describes the next step on the Hero's Journey as the belly of the whale. Here, the hero steps forward into a new experience or place where he or she faces psychological fears of such depth and intensity that these fears feel like a matter of life and death. This is important because confronting those fears is a necessary path to rebirth. And like so many myths from cultures all over the world, the way to achieve redemption and new life is by first walking through hell.

The metaphor of the whale is not accidental. The hero finds him- or herself in the sea, which is a symbol of the psyche or soul. But massive psychological integration, growth, and maturation is not limited to the abstract or the mythical. Indeed, myths exist to illuminate universal human experiences. To reiterate: we all take the Hero's Journey. We can do it intentionally and consciously, or we can do it "accidentally" through being directed by the unconscious. We can let go or be dragged; swim or sink. When we choose the former route, we have options. In lucid dream work we tap into an ancient form of spiritual and psychological self-development through which we can instantly reach worlds, parts of ourselves, and a sense of self-agency that can take years to acquire in a church or a therapist's office. In dreaming, the belly of the whale moment is most commonly found in early sleep phases, when sleep paralysis and hypnagogic hallucinations can contribute to dreams of dying or of falling into an abyss. The belly of the whale is an impossible moment, when we're caught between two worlds to confront the loneliness and darkness that awaits us all in sleep. Such moments can come with dream visions of beings that seem custom designed (because they are, by your own unique subconscious) to trigger the exact emotions that the dreamer needs to feel most.

> *A girl stands at the base of my bed looking at me. She touches my feet; I can't move.*
>
> *I lie awake and see my wife standing next to my bed. That's odd: I didn't hear her get up. She's holding a red blow horn. Quickly she comes toward me and blows the horn in my face. I wake up.*
>
> *I can't move, and I don't feel myself breathing. I close my eyes but can see through my eyelids. I pull the blankets over my head but still see through them. I feel as if I've died.*

Dreams like this commingle the physiological experience of sleep paralysis with the hypnagogic state, producing dreamlike visions. In this state we seem more open than usual to the thoughts and feelings that hit our vulnerable spots: Am I safe? Will this person hurt me if I can't defend myself or escape? Will I die if I let myself fall asleep completely? Dreams can provide, if not answers, at least a way to see the vulnerable spots and stop worry.

In dreams like this the lesson is to give up the desire for control and let the experience happen, to let go into the experience rather than be dragged through it. Of this motif Campbell wrote, "The passage of the threshold is a form of self-annihilation. Instead of passing outward, beyond the confines of the visible world, the hero goes inward, to be born again."

Sometimes we do die in the dream world in order to overcome a fear of death:

A group of us is held up in a house. Zombies are attacking us from outside. Inside, we agree that if one of us is bitten, the others are allowed to kill that person. I get bitten and start turning into a zombie. I do not want to die, but I have an agreement with the others, who point a gun at my head and pull the trigger. I feel part of my face blow off. I feel blood and energy leaving my body, and I pass away into darkness.

Please note that it is rare to allow and to witness a dream in which we actually die. We all have dreams in which we almost die or are about to die, and suddenly wake up or simply don't remember the dream. Death, after all, is one of the ultimate fears, and our lizard brains are activated during sleep in a way that is closely attuned to staying alive. It is for this reason that you don't typically need to fear actual physical harm if you find yourself in the middle of a death dream.

Let me be perfectly clear: we are not chasing after death here. Rather, we are seeking the liberation that can come from untangling ourselves, consciously and unconsciously, from our deepest fears and longings.

When I personally confronted my fear of death, my waking life was transformed. I no longer feared what I didn't understand. I stopped trying to control my dreams or anything else that was out of my control. This transition took years of dreaming and dream journaling, and it was worth it. Diving into the belly of the whale made me ready for the trials ahead.

23
The Road of Trials

Once we have faced the Guardian of the Threshold, once we've subdued the ego and succumbed to going on the Hero's Journey, once we've dived into the abyss and come to terms with our vulnerabilities, still even more trials await. But what a gift! Trials force us to make decisions, and that means that all is not hopeless and beyond our control.

Often we see choices as right or wrong, leading to either success or failure. On the road of trials, choices come both to test us and to help us overcome aspects of ourselves that hold us back. In the process we learn that trials are sometimes meant to be failed. We get many chances—and that's the point. Failing repeatedly is the way to learn and eventually move forward.

Dream trials focus more intensely on the dissolution of the ego and sense of self:

A small girl gives me a small golden key. In front of me, I notice an old, weathered door covered in moss. I walk over to the door, and the key fits perfectly into the lock. The massive stone door opens vertically. I walk through the doorway, and a man is waiting on the other side. I ask him, "Is this the doorway to the future and the past?" He says yes, and I move along.

As soon as I enter, the scenery changes into a psychedelic, kaleidoscopic world. Everything nearby is moving in unison, but in the distance it moves in a disjointed, hectic way. An object moves toward me; I become more and more frightened as it gets closer. I try to get away, but suddenly I'm weightless and just float like an astronaut in the void of space. I wake up.

This image-filled dream starts with the delicate gold key; this is a symbol of how precious the impending journey will be, as well as the symbolic importance of what is required to unlock the Self. Compare the key to what it unlocks—an old, corroded doorway (a portal), which says this journey has been waiting a long time. And according to the gatekeeper, the journey is universal, existing outside of time. In this confusing astral plane, the archetype of the Self awaits. Here's the trial: Does the dreamer meet the true self?

EMOTIONS AS GUIDEPOSTS

When we fail a test that arrives in a dream, you can bet that the same test will present itself again, giving you as many opportunities as you need to pass. It helps to step back and identify what's getting in the way by noticing, while lucid or while fully awake, what emotions are triggered at the point just before you fail the test. Are you experiencing fear? Anger? Grief? This reflection helps you to practice taking a step back from the feeling when you face a trial in a dream and diminishes that feeling in those moments. The road of trials is there to teach us the important lesson that, through repetitive experiences of working to address our failures and fears, we can become better than we already are.

The ground is gray and soft. I look toward the sky and see only velvet darkness. In the distance, there is a mirror about twice my height. I walk over to it, hoping to see something important. I just see my reflection. I look down and see a box. I pick it up; it's some kind of puzzle. I spend a few moments trying to open it and then wake up feeling as though I missed the opportunity to see my higher self in the mirror.

In a separate dream, I'm in my room at night. I sense having an out-of-body experience and decide to travel to visit a friend. I feel pulled downward into the ground and start to feel hot. I'm near the center of the Earth, getting closer and closer until I start to fear I might burn up, physically or spiritually. I stop to rest, then try again. The heat and fear of death overwhelm me, and I wake up.

The road of trials is about overcoming the obstacles that hold us down. These challenges are like the wicked fairies of legend who, as Jung stated, "infatuate the lonely wanderer and lead him astray." In the grand scheme of life, the biggest threat to our well-being is death. Many fight, resist, or fear death, despite its inevitability. This struggle is simply not the way. Coming into contact with death and our fears of dying helps release us from the illusion of control over our lives, and in doing so we release ourselves from fear and anxiety. The courage this release brings will enable us to overcome even bigger obstacles—the Mother and Father—as we continue forward.

24
Anima

Meeting the Goddess

Virtually all mythologies throughout human history tell stories about the hero meeting a goddess, a woman who completes the hero and meets all his desires. These stories are often filled with imagery of love and compassion. The goddess can also represent the perfect picture of the Earth Mother, the one true love we all came from and will return to, but that is only one version of many.

For each of the many stories depicting the divine feminine as harmonious, accepting, kind, and creative, there are just as many that portray her as aggressive, jealous, unfaithful, and destructive. The Greek divinities Hera, whose jealousy and vengefulness is legendary, and Athena, who started the Trojan War after being snubbed by the warrior Paris in a beauty contest, are just two examples of irritable and irrational female behavior in Western mythology. At the same time, many other myths focus on positive traits such as Hera's power and Athena's wisdom.

Our own divine feminine is an amalgamation of the universal depictions of the goddess, both positive and negative, as well as their representations from our earliest lives that live on in the psyche. Known as the *anima,* this feminine aspect of ourselves is made up of mothers, grandmothers, sisters, daughters, aunts, female teachers, and any beings associated with our femininity. In all of us, but particularly in men, the divine not only demands to be seen and integrated, but represents an integration of the psyche that we ignore at our peril.

I see a woman standing by the window. A golden aura of divinity shines from her. I walk over and feel completely accepted, as if I have known her my whole life. She takes my hand and pulls me through the window into another world. There are crowds of people, and she easily passes through them until we arrive at a kind of platform or wall that seems to cross the whole area like a translucent, shimmering field. We pass through too fast for me to comprehend it. She leads me to another group of people—they seem much less alive than the last group. I get a creepy sense that I'm amidst the undead. The golden lady is gone, and I am alone with them. They approach me and hold me, and I feel they're trying to suck the life force from my being. I try to run or fly away, but they grab hold of me. I kick, determined to get away, and finally break free.

Jung talked extensively about the anima within the creative unconscious and how shining a light on it can drastically change our internal worlds for the better. My dream overtly pierces the boundary between the conscious and the unconscious and offers a glimpse of the horrors that reside there. Though terrifying to experience, I believe that the crowds of undead people were not guardians bent on destroying my ego. Rather, the divine feminine aspect of my unconscious, my anima, led me into a scenario with the clear message that my psychic energy was being depleted through committing to too many projects.

An encounter with the anima in dreams also serves as a reminder about the ultimate value and purpose of a dream practice. It's easy to become excessively focused on the goal of lucid dreaming and to continuously reality-check to test our own proficiency. In my case, at the time I had this particular dream I was pushing myself to have as many out-of-body experiences as possible. This sort of aggressive competition with the self, this macho push toward more, is a decidedly masculine path to follow. My dream was a clear message to relax, to allow insights to arise unbidden, and to trust the process and the self. Isn't it funny how such supportive messages can often initially feel frightening? This is a clear example of how an overemphasis on classically masculine traits can hurt us as we try to know the Self and integrate the psyche.

The dream also came with a decisive road of trials moment when the goddess left. Ironically, her departure left me with a reminder that we are responsible for independently making difficult decisions in the dream world just as we are in waking life. Therefore, we need to take the dream world seriously, not as a competition to be won or a space to be mastered by brute force and control. Rather, we benefit most when we treat what we find in dreams with the reverence, humility, and gracious acceptance that we can acquire by tapping into our divine feminine nature.

Finally, this rich dream shows us that the world of the unconscious is vaster and more powerful than any conscious understanding. "The unconscious is an autonomous psychic entity," Jung wrote. "Any efforts to drill it are only apparently successful, and moreover are harmful to the consciousness." He warns anyone trying to control the creative aspects of their minds that "we can listen but may not meddle." While exercising some control over the dream world is implicit in any lucid dreaming practice, it's important to remember that manipulating objects and scenery, or hitting a target for how many times you have a lucid dream, misses the point and can actually diminish the value of the dream world. Developing the skill of lucid dreaming is no small feat, but if you can release yourself from external metrics of success and truly look at the dream world, you will quickly realize that you cannot control it, just as you cannot control the waking world.

If, as is commonly done, we look at the dream world as a sort of video game, then we can see much more easily that the dream environment is not something we create through our choices. Rather, this world is continually created around us, and our choices and their results are responses to the environment. So wherever we go in a dream, our unconscious mind has already been there. Because of that, the narrator or observer of the dream world knows what, where, and who we will see before we choose to manifest or move forward. The result is the illusion of control over the unconscious. But the dream is always one step ahead of us. Jung said it best in his essay "General Aspects of Dream Psychology" when he implied that we are all parts of the dream simultaneously. "This whole creation is essentially subjective, and the dream is the theater where the dreamer is at once scene, actor, prompter, stage manager, author, audience, and critic."

25
Animus

Atonement with the Father

An **atonement** is often depicted as the act of reparation for wrongdoings or sins. In the Bible's Old Testament, individuals sacrificed valuable animals or gave up other important possessions in order to make things right with their god. In the Christian New Testament, Jesus is crucified, offering himself as a universal atonement for the sins of humankind. So in some of the earliest religious narratives, there is an intertwining of sin—the separation of self from source—and atonement that leads to reunification with the Father. Acts of atonement in the form of sacrifice clean the soul and make way for the true self to emerge, like a snake shedding its skin or the Ouroboros eternally consuming itself.

When we dream within the Hero's Journey framework, we have repeated opportunities to clean up the fractured aspects of the Self and realign them into something new and improved. Just as sleep offers physical healing and regeneration, our dreams offer mental and emotional healing. Over time, our nightly atonements add up to a psychological journey of much greater magnitude. In dreams we practice—in the classical meaning of devoted, repetitive, and thoughtful practice—coming to all the way stations on the Hero's Journey. We undertake the journey; we practice recognizing portals and encountering guardians;

we recognize the anima and other characters and landscapes of the unconscious mind. We continually do the work of overcoming our fears, acknowledging the innumerable hidden aspects of ourselves, and learning our personal dream symbol vocabulary. In the process, we become more and more whole.

Even with years of practice, moments of atonement can be jarring. When I was studying for my master's degree in consciousness and transformative studies, I started to read Jungian scholar Mircea Eliade's book *Shamanism: Archaic Techniques of Ecstasy*. Reading about shamanic initiations across cultures, I recognized links between sacrifice, transcendence, and the image of the Father or the Divine Masculine. Initiates are typically taken from their homes by men, often in reality but commonly in dreams, transported to either heaven or to the underworld, and then cut into pieces and reassembled. The parallels between shamanic initiations, lucid dreaming, out-of-body experiences, and Jung's anima/animus integration are apparent. However the experiences are framed by different cultures and methods, in the end it remains the classic theme of transformation.

This process of resurrection—atonement, descent, disintegration, and reintegration—is the ultimate experience for the shaman, the Jungian, and the oneironaut alike. Setting the intention of a willingness to transform opens the door for transformation to arrive.

In the following dream, notice the surroundings, the guardian, and the mode of transport.

It's dark, and I'm free falling and floating into my bed. I see a light, and I experience myself outside of my body. I fly out the window to a large space where I'm surrounded by ski lifts. I walk toward a man, and he waves at me. He explains that he's been waiting for me for some time. "Are you ready?" he asks. I say I am, and he puts me on one of the lifts. I am immediately transported to an old house, where I am standing in a hallway. There's a kitchen light in the distance. Just as I feel a powerful presence in front of me, a man appears—he's at least seven feet tall. I know what he wants, so I follow him to a room.

I stand there as he moves me to different positions around the room using only his mind. At one point I'm lying under him. He takes out a large knife and starts cutting at my body. He saws off my arms, my legs, and eventually my head. I feel pain, but I don't resist. As soon as he finishes, I'm back in one piece and all is well. I wake up.

A dream like this—while it's easy to say it's informed by the material I'd been reading in the conscious world—marks a new level of reintegration, the completion of a process. When we allow ourselves to experience dreams like this, a key turns, and the door separating us from our higher selves is unlocked.

26
The Reward
A Reflection

When heroes are at the moment of reward, they can look back and see how all the people, events, and learning along the journey conspired to get them to this point. Heroes see the journey not as an event that took place but as a cumulative snapshot of their entire life. A moment of enlightenment may feel like just that—a sudden understanding of everything—but that moment is only the next step on a long path. So the moment of reward on the Hero's Journey, while it is an ending of sorts, is not *the* end. It's simply another point on the map.

On my personal journey, the reward was a sudden clarity about why I was exploring dreams in the first place. I had always been fascinated by my dreams, and when I started to actively work with my dreams, something inside me drove an intense desire to keep exploring. It was as if my soul were calling me. Over time, reflecting on and truly listening to my dreams led me to a moment of epiphany about their purpose: dreams are here to help us find our true selves.

Ironically, this discovery, and the journey that led me to it, has had at least as significant an impact on my waking life as it has on my dream practice. I often find myself in waking situations where I pause and take a moment to simply observe. In the dream world I react exactly the same way. Both of these reactions are a result of lucid dreaming techniques. And just as I've learned to make choices and adapt in the dream world, I've learned to do the same in everyday life.

A key component of what makes this moment of pause remarkable and invaluable in life is its ability to help identify emotions from moment to moment. Understanding and then facing fears was the most transformational aspect of my dream work. Fear fractures us into smaller and smaller portions as we disassociate from those fears. If we can parse dream monsters and phantoms as fears in our waking lives, and put these fears away in boxes in the unconscious, we no longer have to see them as a part of ourselves. Rather, we can then treat our fears as something other that we can hate, reject, or ignore.

As well, by facing these fears, we develop the courage to be accountable for who we are, in all of our beauty and hideousness. We face the horrors we are capable of. Once we clearly see the darker aspects we keep buried in the personal and collective unconscious, we grow past them, look at them squarely, let them dismantle us, and become whole again. We reemerge as more mature individuals.

I want to stress the fear factor for a minute, in case my account makes it sound too easy. Fear is powerful; there's a reason that "Do not let your hearts be troubled and do not be afraid" is such a popular Bible verse. Humans are mammals hardwired for safety, so we are highly attuned to danger and fear. This is a primal force that lives deep within our collective and individual unconscious. Fear isn't something that humans can simply eradicate, so it's important—but difficult—to learn how to manage it.

Personally, I struggled with the fear of death. I feared the fact of death, like most of us do, but it also was intensely upsetting for me to think about what happens after we die. Some might say that lucid dreaming and out-of-body experiences are enough evidence to believe in the afterlife, but the contrary is true for me. It just told me that any reality is plausible; heaven and hell are symbolic realms created by our collective imagination in an effort to explain the inexplicable. Believing in any particular afterlife generated anxiety about death much the same way that my religious background did. But dream work reminds us that extinguishing our essential self—which I believe contains the core fear of death—is simply not possible. Consciousness lives in us and beyond us. Dream work allows us to relinquish the desire to control the fact of death and to identify the aspects of ourselves that are hidden from the waking consciousness. That's all I need to understand.

Additionally, I had significant anxiety and fear around my identity. We're all fundamentally selfish and capable of inflicting incredible damage in the right (or wrong) circumstances. To ignore those darker aspects of ourselves is like having an alternative personality hidden from everyone's view—including our own. That shadow will inevitably demand to be seen. Again, it's a case of let go or be dragged along.

Merging with my shadow allowed me to identify with the parts of myself that I don't necessarily like. Beyond that, dream work gave me a frame to treat those parts like any other aspect of my personality rather than as the enemy that Jung depicted. "We simply accuse our enemy of our own unadmitted faults." Merging with the shadow is looking into the mirror of our own faults, becoming human, and humbling ourselves. Nightmares and horrible dreams are doing their best to convey this message and to teach us that in order to achieve greatness, you also need darkness. By destroying or ignoring one, you limit the other.

The reward of this merging of our disparate selves is kindness, understanding, and compassion for the Self and for others. That seems to be the reason that facing the Guardian of the Threshold may not be a one-off experience. Dreams may ask us to confront the Guardian of the Threshold over and over: every encounter with the shadow increases our ability to face ourselves.

Identifying with the anima in the dream of the goddess allowed me to interact with some of the more unconscious aspects of myself. Crossing through the veil into the land of the dead was a metaphorical representation of how I treated my creative feminine nature, tucked away and hidden from daily life. Through dreams, I could experience some of the suffering that this hiding away had created, and I was able to make better choices. Confronting the Father, going through the atonement of being cut apart and made anew, also cut away the parts of me that somehow had been displaced and disfigured and realigned them into a cohesive body. This intense atonement, experienced through lucid dreams, changed who I was from that point on.

In summation, it is clear that dreaming is not so different from waking life. They are both journeys, or simulations, that manifest out of our ideas and beliefs, both individual and collective. Dreams change as beliefs change. We can bring our conscious mind into the dream space to mingle with those parts of ourselves that are tethered to something much greater. Though this may seem powerful and at first exhilarating, we soon learn that the real power of lucid dreaming comes from surrender.

While all aspects of our consciousness may feel true or real, when we examine them more closely under the lens of lucid dreaming, we see that they may be an illusion—this is true for fear, death, life, and dreaming. These concepts are all aspects of the same thing, are all shards flowing out of the shattered consciousness. In order to get past the illusion of reality, you must go on the journey—past our ideas about reality, past our symbolic representations of ourselves, and into the heart of the true self.

PART 5

◆ ◆ ◆

Advanced Tools and Supplements for Lucid Dreaming

27

Lucid Dreaming
Supplements

As we go deeper into this work, we inevitably come up against the reality that lucid dreaming is not easy. Just as in most other areas of life, it's tempting to wish for a magic pill to get us there faster and more easily, even if we know that dedication and effort lead to a more rewarding experience. Fortunately, there is an array of supplements that can help us dream lucidly without shirking the hard work.

Lucid dreamers looking for nutritional or herbal assistance are in luck. Many naturally occurring substances can gently and effectively aid in producing and improving lucid dreams by enhancing the mind's normal processes during sleep. Some can increase REM sleep; others can improve awareness and memory. Many are common vitamins and herbs that are available over the counter; you may already consume them in food, tea, or supplements. Others have been used in religious ceremonies for thousands of years. After years of self-exploration, reading peer-reviewed documents about supplements and books on lucid dreaming, I've discovered which of the options work best and compiled them here. I hope this will save you money and time when finding out what works for you.

A word of caution: some of these supplements can be quite powerful, illegal, or veiled in stigma. Mixing and matching substances can also be dangerous. Prolonged use may affect the body in unexpected ways, and what is safe for one person isn't always safe for another. Please check with a health care provider before taking any of these, especially if you're taking medications, as they may interact with any of the supplements listed.

FINDING A PLACE TO START

When considering a lucid dreaming supplement, the two most important priorities are improving the dream state and building awareness. Therefore, we want supplements that help us relax, increase the time spent in REM, improve memory recall, and maximize our control while dreaming. The following are aids that are especially good for each of these goals.

Relaxing and Getting to Bed

If you're like many oneironauts, excited to start lucid dreaming, then getting relaxed enough to sleep may present the first obstacle. A supplement that can help us to fall asleep quickly and naturally will also effectively promote lucid dreaming. The best natural sleep aids happen to be both affordable and available at nearly every pharmacy or health food store.

Melatonin

Produced by the pineal gland of the brain, this hormone increases as it gets dark and thus regulates our circadian rhythms. Today, though, the twenty-four-hour light from computer screens, traffic, and all the conveniences of modern life can make it hard for the brain to produce enough melatonin to maintain a healthy circadian rhythm. Taking a small amount of melatonin as a supplement can be a safe and effective way to relax, fall asleep more quickly, and also feel more rested when we do wake up.

Valerian Root and Lemon Balm

These traditional plant remedies have been used to aid relaxation and sleep for generations. Valerian root and lemon balm are mild, safe, and effective calming herbs found in many sleep-support teas and can also be purchased in liquid and capsule forms. Valerian root on its own has a notoriously unpleasant musty scent and flavor, but there are many popular tea blends that contain an effective amount of the root. Lemon balm tastes lemony, just as its name suggests.

Increasing REM

Although humans dream four to five times each night during REM cycles that occur roughly every ninety minutes, research has found that pushing REM to later in the sleep session can make dreams more vivid and help us remember them better. A lucid dreaming pill that can push REM to later parts of the night can be quite effective when it comes to remembering our dreams, and there are a few that can do just that.

5-HTP

5-HTP is the single most effective lucid dreaming supplement for increasing dream recall. This amino acid gets converted in the brain to serotonin, which (among its many functions) has been shown to push REM to later parts of the night.

Mugwort (*Artemisia vulgaris*)

Just like 5-HTP, mugwort has been shown to increase REM activity later in the night and to allow for better dream recall. There are many species of mugwort, so it's essential to use the correct species as only *Artemisia vulgaris* does the job.

Increasing Awareness while Dreaming and Improving Memory Recall

Most of us forget our dreams soon after waking up. We often remember that we had a dream but find it difficult to recall many aspects of it. The more time that passes, the less of the dream we remember. Herbs and supplements that are shown to increase memory recall can help us remember our dreams, lucid or not. Surprisingly, two highly effective memory supplements also may offer an advantage when it comes to getting lucid.

Alpha-GPC

This nootropic supplement is popular in the United States to improve memory, concentration, and learning, but in Europe it's prescribed for the treatment of Alzheimer's disease. Taken on its own, alpha-GPC is less effective than just galantamine alone. When used in combination with galantamine, it can extend the effects of galantamine to improve dream control and awareness.

Galantamine

Galantamine, the only lucid dreaming supplement with peer-reviewed research to establish its effectiveness, has been shown to substantially increase both memory recall and dream awareness. As a lucid dreaming aid, galantamine is so powerful that many people start lucid dreaming after a single dose.

THE COMPLETE LIST

Sleep and lucid dreaming primarily involve the neurotransmitters acetylcholine, serotonin, and GABA. These three influence sleep quality as well as dream memory and vividness. This list is divided into those functions as much as possible, but you'll see that many recommended supplements span multiple categories.

Supplements to Improve Sleep Quality

Ashwagandha

Known as Indian ginseng, ashwagandha has been used to help individuals with troubled sleep for thousands of years and has sedating effects similar to melatonin. It also may increase the number of dreams you have throughout the night. Though not much has been known about why ashwagandha improves sleep induction and dream recall, recent research may have uncovered useful evidence. Triethylene glycol, a chemical found in ashwagandha, has induced sleep and increased REM in rats. This would explain the herb's effects on dream recall.

How to Use It: Take ashwagandha just before bed to take advantage of its sedative potential. For dream recall, it's best used in conjunction with a Wake Back to Bed (WBTB) method. Ashwagandha can be found at your local health food store or in some teas.

Calea ternifolia

Used by preconquest indigenous Mexican peoples as a ceremonial herb to talk with ancestors while asleep, today it is often used in lucid dreaming supplements for its ability to induce sleep. There is little research currently available on *Calea ternifolia*. It seems to help people fall asleep much faster than they would without it; it may also improve dream recall and spontaneous awakenings.

How to Use It: Take at bedtime to promote sleep onset, allow for more vivid hypnagogic visuals, and improve dream recall. A high dose of *Calea ternifolia* is not recommended, as it can cause nausea and diarrhea. If you do end up using this supplement, start with a very low amount and work up so that you do not overdo it. Dosages depend on body type, so continue with your own research to find a dose that works for you.

Chamomile Flower

Chamomile flower can help us get to sleep faster so that we can start to dream sooner. Another common use for chamomile is to calm the mind after a stressful day. Since focus and paying attention to our non-thought processes are helpful in having lucid dreams and out-of-body experiences, chamomile flower is one of the most powerful and popular herbs used to calm the body. Its effectiveness in helping sleep come more quickly is on par with that of many medications.

How to Use It: Have some chamomile tea roughly thirty minutes before sleep. This will ensure that you have absorbed the active components of the tea.

L-taurine

L-taurine is an essential amino acid that helps control fat in the human body. There is some research into its effects on the hippocampus, but it is still unclear how this supplement may calm the nervous system. L-taurine most likely affects the brain's GABA receptors, but researchers have yet to determine the exact mechanism. Anecdotally, L-taurine functions as a sleep aid and increases dreams. It seems to help with getting to sleep more quickly and increasing feelings of restfulness.

How to Use It: Taken in capsule form thirty to forty minutes before bed makes it likely you'll enjoy a restful sleep. L-taurine becomes a very powerful lucid dreaming supplement on nights that rest is needed.

Melatonin

Melatonin is a natural hormone produced in the pineal gland, where it is converted from serotonin once the environment gets dark. Even scant amounts of light have been shown to completely stop the brain's natural production of melatonin. Melatonin as a supplement can help reduce the time it takes for sleep onset, improve sleep quality, and make dreams more vivid and realistic. It may also interfere with the process of turning serotonin into melatonin, which would push REM to later in the sleep cycle. Overall, melatonin is shown to have long-lasting positive effects on sleep.

How to Use It: Take melatonin at bedtime. Melatonin may be the most helpful supplement if light is unavoidable in your sleep area. Implementing environmental changes—such as keeping the bedroom completely dark, wearing a sleep mask, or similar fixes—can also support melatonin production and help you feel sleepy.

Niacin

Niacin is an essential vitamin that is required by the human body. Most of us get enough niacin from coffee and niacin-fortified foods to stay reasonably healthy. However, in higher doses niacin offers important benefits. It may also help to improve sleep on restless nights. A 500-milligram dose of niacin releases a protein called PGD2, considered the most potent sleep aid known to humankind. In fact, this protein may even be a primary instigator of sleep. A niacin flush, which will take place ten to fifteen minutes after ingestion, helps the body relax and fall asleep; common side effects are sensations of warmth and itching, but they fade quickly.

How to Use It: Take the label-recommended dosage before going to sleep every other night. Niacin is a powerful lucid dreaming supplement, best used on break nights from lucid dreaming to ensure good rest.

Passion Flower

Although passion flower has not been studied extensively, the small amount of extant research aligns with its traditional reputation as a sleep aid and anxiety reducer. Getting to sleep more quickly and calming down the mind can help with focus and attention in lucid dreaming, as well as help you get to sleep faster.

How to Use It: Take passion flower in a tea at least thirty minutes before going to bed to ensure complete absorption.

Valerian Root and Lemon Balm

Valerian root and lemon balm are grouped together because they are both mild sedatives. Valerian root is one of the most common sedatives, often found in sleep-supporting tea blends (alone, valerian smells and tastes pretty bad). Lemon balm has similar effects, but with better flavor. Together these herbs support more relaxing and restful sleep by helping to release muscle tension.

How to Use It: In tea or pill form, take just before lying down to sleep.

Supplements to Improve Dream Memory Recall

5-HTP and Magnesium Glycinate

5-HTP and magnesium glycinate may push REM sleep to later in the night, increasing the chance that we'll remember our dreams when we wake up in the morning. This is because 5-HTP and magnesium glycinate are precursors to serotonin in that they are later converted into serotonin by the body. Magnesium is involved in wakefulness and memory. When brain serotonin levels rise during sleep, acetylcholine levels are commonly suppressed, allowing for later periods of REM.

When REM sleep is pushed later, those REM periods may include more dreams than normal during a short period of time (known as REM rebound). Higher acetylcholine levels at this time may help us remember dreams better. Compare it to a long night of drinking: alcohol releases serotonin into the brain and represses acetylcholine. Once the alcohol wears off, you may wake up remembering vivid dreams. The impact on health and comfort are quite different, but the mechanism and effects are similar.

How to Use It: Take before bed. However, if you are trying to remember non-REM dreams such as out-of-body experiences, you could use them during the day, then set an alarm for several hours later when the 5-HTP has worn off.

African Dream Herb (*Silene undulata*)

In many traditions throughout southern and eastern Africa, this plant has been used in shamanic practices, especially while dreaming. There is little available research about *Silene undulata*, but some reports suggest that it has been used to induce vivid dreams. It also seems to affect hypnagogic visuals prior to sleep, similar to the effects of *Calea ternifolia*. Like its Mexican counterpart, it may act by disrupting REM sleep and increasing REM rebound.

How to Use It: Use prior to sleep. Stir a tablespoon of the powdered root into about one liter of water until a thick foam forms. Drink the foam. Alternatively, stir the powdered or chopped roots into boiling water and steep into a tea.

Choline: Choline Bitartrate, Alpha-GPC, and CDP-Choline

Choline bitartrate, alpha-GPC, and CDP-choline are key lucid dreaming herbs for their role in improving memory. All three are precursors to choline, which is a precursor to acetylcholine. Choline precursors increase acetylcholine in the brain, which in turn enhances general memory, increases the length of REM periods, and improves dream memory recall. It seems that alpha-GPC is the best of the three, as it has been shown to be more effective in turning into acetylcholine and crossing the blood-brain barrier.

How to Use It: It is best to use choline precursors later at night. Using the WBTB method, in which you set an alarm and then go back to bed, in conjunction with taking a supplement before going back to bed, such as choline bitartrate and alpha-GPC, is another option. There may be no bad time to take choline bitartrate and alpha-GPC unless you have trouble going to sleep. Remember that serotonin and acetylcholine are in charge of your sleep-wake cycle, so taking an acetylcholine precursor could increase your wakefulness as well. It takes about three hours for the body to process alpha-GPC into the chemicals needed to improve dream recall, so keep that in mind when using.

GABA

GABA is a neurotransmitter involved in many basic functions, such as motor control and vision; it also has a role in regulating anxiety, presumably by reducing the overall excitability of neurons. The more GABA there is in the brain during sleep, the less REM there seems to be. The presence of GABA also may inhibit memory. These seem like pretty non-dream-supportive effects, but taken as a supplement it can also relax the mind enough to improve non-REM sleep, giving us a better chance of achieving higher-quality REM states as well. It has also been found to improve sleep quality without causing unwanted drowsiness, improve non-REM sleep quality, and increase brain-activated behavioral states during dreaming. Most of the current research says that GABA doesn't cross the blood-brain barrier in humans, but my personal experience and anecdotal evidence suggest otherwise, as many dreamers have used this supplement successfully.

How to Use It: Take well before going to bed—up to a few hours prior—so that its effects are waning around the time you anticipate a REM stage. This appears to be the most effective way to provide restful sleep, push REM into later in the night, and increase the odds that you'll remember your dreams.

Galantamine

This supplement is a hidden gem for improving cognitive awareness, dream quality, working memory, and memory recall. You might think of galantamine as a powerful booster for glutamate, which is an excitatory neurotransmitter that affects cognition and memory. Researchers speculate that this is because galantamine enhances acetylcholine receptors, which in turn increases glutamate transmission in the brain (see studies by Penner and Sparrow). With daily dosages of eight milligrams, increased to sixteen milligrams after three months, Alzheimer's patients showed increased cognitive performance. In nonclinical use, galantamine helps significantly in noticing and recalling dreams. Unlike GABA, which depresses the nervous system and reduces memory recall in exchange for a mind relaxed enough to notice and remember dreams, galantamine puts the brain in a state that can remain aware of what's happening while dreaming.

How to Use It: The best way to use galantamine is with the WBTB method. Sleep for about four to five hours, then take the package-suggested dose. Allow forty-eight hours between doses to avoid building a tolerance. Galantamine can increase focus while dreaming and is one of the most powerful lucid dreaming supplements available. The flip side is that it causes a mental alertness that can make it hard to get back to sleep.

Guayusa

Guayusa is made from *Ilex guayusa,* a holly tree native to the Amazon region of South America. A stimulant, it is usually brewed as a tea in water and used after waking as a morning pick-me-up and to improve memory recall. As Stefan Zugo describes, there is some evidence that guayusa is more effective in dream recall than coffee or a placebo because it provides more focused calm.

How to Use It: Make it as a tea and drink after sleeping, preferably in conjunction with the WBTB method. You can also take it before bed, but it may increase your awareness to the point that it can be hard to go back to sleep. Make sure you're not prone to insomnia before using it in this way.

Huperzine-A

Huperzine-A increases the amount of REM sleep we have throughout the night. It also interrupts enzymes in the brain that normally would break down acetylcholine. As a result, it promotes a buildup of acetylcholine, thus increasing our recall of events and impressions and improving memory formation and recall.

How to Use It: Use as part of a WBTB method to take advantage of the acetylcholine buildup that will have taken place naturally during sleep. By this time, your serotonin levels should have dropped, allowing for more REM when you go back to sleep.

Lion's Mane

Lion's mane, or *Hericium erinaceus,* is a white, globe-shaped mushroom covered with long, shaggy spines (looking very much like its name would suggest). It has long been used as a naturopathic remedy to reduce pain and improve heart and brain health. The fungus has powerful antioxidant properties and may help treat diabetes, heart disease, autoimmune disorders, and other chronic ailments associated with the typical modern Western lifestyle. It may also significantly improve memory and cognitive function. Recently, lion's mane has been the subject of research studies that back up its traditional claims. This research suggests that lion's mane regrows the myelin sheaths in the brain, strengthening communication between neurons, and can remove the myelin sheath plaque believed to be the cause of Alzheimer's. As a lucid dreaming supplement, lion's mane can help us to remain lucid while dreaming and to remember what we've witnessed during sleep. Some dreamers also report having more vivid dreams.

How to Use It: Mycologist, author, and mushroom guru Paul Stamets recommends two milliliters daily (split into two doses) to improve cognitive function. He also suggests combining lion's mane with niacin to enhance effectiveness.

L-theanine

The amino acid L-theanine blocks the production of glutamate, allowing for higher levels of GABA to be present in the brain. As GABA increases, we feel drowsy, the central nervous system relaxes, and sleep comes more easily. When L-theanine wears off, the remaining glutamate may result in more vivid dreams and improved awareness and recall. In combination with other GABA-opposing supplements, L-theanine can become an extremely powerful lucid dreaming supplement.

How to Use It: Take the label-recommended supplement dosage at bedtime. If your goal is to have vivid dreams right at the point of sleep, use L-theanine five to six hours before sleep. You may feel drowsy or forgetful during this time.

Marijuana (*Cannabis sativa* or *Cannabis indica*)

Marijuana's place in the lucid dreamer's arsenal is often misunderstood because many users have a hard time remembering their dreams. This is not because of the plant, which is actually a highly effective acetylcholinesterase inhibitor and GABA activator. Marijuana has a six-hour half-life, so the increase in GABA during this time would reduce memory formation and memory recall. However, marijuana can improve memory as GABA levels drop. Using marijuana sparingly will not only improve your ability to dream but could also strengthen memory formation. When dream recall is a problem, it's usually because the plant is smoked or ingested close to bedtime. Marijuana also does not stop REM, another common myth. I've noticed in my own personal use that cannabidiol (CBD), which is related to cannabis, is also useful for promoting relaxation in order to have better sleep but does not affect the brain the same as cannabis and is not as useful as a tool.

How to Use It: To ensure enough time between use and its memory-enhancing effect, use a small amount of marijuana in the morning. Additionally, heavier use (at any time of day) followed by a break of two to three days would give a similar effect.

Mexican Dream Herb (*Calea ternifolia*)

This herb has long been used in indigenous Mexican culture to bring visions during sleep. The way *Calea ternifolia* acts in the brain is unknown, but it may impact GABA or disrupt REM sleep, as it produces sensations of drowsiness and forgetfulness upon ingestion and seems to enhance dream recall as it wears off.

How to Use It: Use before going to sleep or early on in the night. It may be taken as a tea or smoked. This will maximize the REM rebound effect upon waking.

Mugwort (*Artemisia vulgaris*)

Mugwort is a bitter-tasting herb that, in addition to being a powerful lucid dreaming aid, is also used in brewing beer. This humble plant seems to improve sleep onset and affect serotonin and GABA levels in the brain. Mugwort can improve awakening early on in the sleep cycle, help induce out-of-body experiences, and enhance vibrational stages of out-of-body experiences. It also affects memory of dreams due to its relationship to the GABA neurotransmitter.

How to Use It: Because mugwort is not pleasant to taste and is in fact quite bitter, I recommend taking mugwort extract in pill form. Use the recommended dose before going to bed to experience lucid awakening as well as vibrational states in out-of-body experiences.

Salvia divinorum

Salvia is a potent psychedelic drug. It can produce extremely intense, even terrifying, hallucinations. Salvia hallucinations are often seen even when the user's eyes are open, and they can appear to interact with reality, making them appear truly real. Furthermore, unlike some other psychedelics, salvia does not produce paralysis. This makes having a chaperone during salvia use highly recommended, if not essential, to keep the user safe. Keeping all that in mind, **if used in very small amounts,** salvia can have a significant impact on our dreams, improve memory recall, and enhance the vividness and intensity of the dreamscape. Salvia interacts with kappa opioid and glutamate receptors in the brain, both of which are key to producing out-of-body experiences.

> **A word of caution: salvia has a reverse tolerance mechanism, so the more you use, the more powerful it gets. Thus, you need less and less to get the same effects. This plant and its extracts may be illegal in your area.**

How to Use It: **with caution.** Choose loose leaf rather than an extract, as extracts can be very powerful and may cause unwanted psychedelic effects. Use salvia before going to bed, in a tea, or in a tincture to be absorbed in the mouth.

Velvet Bean (Mucuna pruriens)

Velvet bean is a wild legume common in tropical and subtropical regions. It has been found to have some of the highest extract rates of L-dopa, a precursor to dopamine, which is important to cognitive function, memory, motor function, reward systems, and dreaming; low levels of dopamine are associated with Parkinson's disease and are also believed to be one of the leading causes of depression. Some research has found that when we dream, the area of the brain right above the eyes is activated—this area is also activated by dopamine. By increasing dopamine levels, velvet bean can lead to more dreams and improved memories of those dreams.

How to Use It: Any substance that increases dopamine can become addictive or cause other harm. Because of this, keep dosages as low as possible and use only intermittently before bed.

Vitamin B6

Vitamin B6 is an essential nutrient that is involved in the production of a number of hormones and neurotransmitters. It has a role in producing histamines and improving adrenal function, which are linked to circadian rhythms, sleep health, and dreaming. Vitamin B6 deficiency has been linked to depression and other negative psychological and neurological effects. Regulating vitamin B6 levels can improve sleep quality and overall memory recall.

How to Use It: Take vitamin B6 during the day on its own, in a B-complex, or in a multivitamin. It takes time for the body to convert vitamin B6 into the hormones and neurotransmitters necessary to help with dreaming. **Do not take in conjunction with 5-HTP as this could overload the system with serotonin.**

Yohimbe (*Pausinystalia johimbe*)

Yohimbe is made from the root bark of the yohimbe tree found in western and central Africa. It is now available in supplement form to support adrenal function. Yohimbe releases chemicals (such as adrenaline) that improve memory formation without disrupting the processes that promote relaxation.

How to Use It: Yohimbe is extremely potent, and you will be quick to build a tolerance. It's best to use the label-recommended dosage of 500 to 750 milligrams within a WBTB practice. Using yohimbe in conjunction with galantamine can enhance the effects of both considerably. Additionally, taking three to four days off after using yohimbe may ensure that tolerance does not build up.

Supplements to Improve Dream Vividness

Reishi Mushroom

Reishi mushroom is a popular ingredient in anti-inflammatory and immune-support supplements, but it's also an excellent lucid dream aid that helps dreams become more vivid. There is little research about how reishi mushroom affects dreams; however, there are numerous anecdotal reports that reishi makes dreams more impactful and even more nightmarish. It could be that the mushroom induces light-sleep non-REM dreaming, which can be conducive to nightmares. When I used reishi mushroom for the physical health benefits, I noticed that my dreams began to take on greater emotional resonance. Reishi may also make dreams more personally meaningful.

How to Use It: Take the label-recommended dose before bed for a long night of impactful and possibly frightful dreams.

28

Supplementing Tips, Plans, and Recipes

Now that you have a long list of lucid dreaming herbs, you're probably wondering, *How do I use all these?* The answer to that question is that you don't want to use them all at once, and sometimes you may not want to use any at all. Think of it like cooking: just as making a healthy meal takes a bit of effort, hard work is essential in dream practice. A diet of convenience may taste good in the short term, but it is no substitute for healthy cooking. Supplements may be useful, but they are no substitute for a well-grounded, deliberate dreaming practice. A similar metaphor can be said regarding rest. Sometimes you want a nice meal before dessert, or you may not want dessert every night. The same goes for sleep. You always need rest before attempting to lucid dream, and sometimes you may just want a good night's rest without engaging in lucid dreaming.

On a more serious note, which I've mentioned already but it is important enough to repeat: it is critical that you use caution when taking any lucid dreaming supplements, alone or in combination. I highly recommend that you speak with your doctor or other medical professional to make sure they are safe for you. Even though most of the supplements I've listed here are easy to find in local grocery or health food stores, they may interact adversely with your individual chemistry or with other medications you may be taking.

Remember, the goal in taking supplements is to enhance the quality of your sleep and dreaming without detracting from your overall well-being. In addition, supplements do not guarantee lucidity; they are merely a tool in a larger practice.

With that, here are four recipes and tips to help you get the most out of your supplement use. Unless specified otherwise, use vitamin and herbal supplement dosages recommended on the product packaging.

FOR A GOOD NIGHT'S REST

- Valerian root or lemon balm—in tea, capsule, or tincture
- 500 milligrams niacin (consult with a doctor to ensure this dosage is right for you; do not use types labeled "flush-free")
- Melatonin as needed for sleep

Take valerian root or lemon balm and niacin before bed. Lie down and rest; allow the flush to wash over you, and then close your eyes and sleep.

Result: you should wake up less often and have fewer stressful dreams. If you feel that you are still stressed out, you can add in melatonin before you go to bed.

FOR LUCID DREAMS

- 500 milligrams niacin (consult with a doctor to ensure this dosage is right for you; do not use types labeled "flush-free")
- 5-HTP
- Mugwort
- Alpha-GPC

Take niacin, 5-HTP, and mugwort before sleep. Wait for restfulness to overcome your body after the niacin flush, and then relax in bed. You can perform the WILD technique and set your alarm to wake up after four hours of sleep. Once you wake up, take the alpha-GPC and go back to sleep.

Result: during this whole process, you will be waking up more often than you have before. The interrupted sleep should move your REM stages to later in the night, improving dream memory.

FOR ADVANCED LUCID DREAMS

- Four milligrams galantamine

Set an alarm for four to five hours from bedtime, and go to sleep. When the alarm goes off, take the galantamine and engage in some light activity for about an hour. Go back to sleep. At that point, you should be fully awake, and going back to sleep should be a challenge. Training yourself to focus on going back to sleep will make this easier.

Result: once you are back asleep you can start to directly enter lucid dreams.

Take forty-eight-hour breaks between each use of this combination.

FOR IMPROVED MEMORY AND COGNITIVE FUNCTION

- 500 milligrams niacin (consult with a doctor to ensure this dosage is right for you; do not use types labeled "flush-free")
- Lion's mane
- Reishi mushroom
- Alpha-GPC

Use these either daily or every other day at bedtime. Alternate use with and without niacin. This will help you to improve overall cognitive function as well as improve your ability to remember your dreams.

Result: this combination will not necessarily help you improve your dream recall, but it will give you a better night's rest. On the nights you are not taking niacin, you should experience greater vividness and recall of your dreams.

29
Galantamine
Lucid Dreaming's Holy Grail?

hen it comes to specifically improving the experience of lucid dreams, galantamine is far and away the most effective supplement. This powerful compound is still fairly new to the medical community and unknown to many laypeople, so it merits its own chapter.

WHAT IS GALANTAMINE?

Galantamine can be produced from the extract of the common snowdrop (*Galanthus nivalis*), the red spider lily (*Lycoris radiata*), other snowdrop varieties, or synthetically. It relieves cognitive dysfunction by increasing levels of acetylcholine, the neurotransmitter involved in memory formation, not only in waking life but also in sleep. Since its discovery in 1947, galantamine has been used primarily to treat Alzheimer's disease. In recent years it's also been used as a supplement to enhance general memory and dream recall.

GALANTAMINE IN LUCID DREAMING

It's hard to say exactly when or how galantamine first started to be used in lucid dreaming, but we can definitively say that it has rapidly gained in popularity among the oneironaut community. Thomas Yuschak wrote about galantamine and its powerful effects in his 2006 book *Advanced Lucid Dreaming: The Power of Supplements.* More recently, the professional research community has begun to rally around galantamine as the possible gold standard of lucid dreaming supplements.

In August 2018, Sparrow and his researchers published an article in the journal *Consciousness and Cognition* showing that galantamine is about 50 percent more likely to induce a lucid dreaming experience in an individual than any other statistically significant lucid dreaming system. A second article, by LaBerge and his research team and also published in 2018, supported these findings.

Because galantamine was effective not only in increasing users' chances of having a lucid dream but also improved—by 50 percent— the likelihood of having a lucid dream regardless of the technique used, it would appear that the chemical effect of increased acetylcholine and glutamate levels in the brain may be a more reliable determinant of lucid dreams than the techniques we might use to encourage them.

GALANTAMINE DREAMS

The power of galantamine to induce lucid dreams is clear; however, what we don't fully understand is how galantamine might affect dream content or quality. Those who use galantamine describe their dreams as more vivid, longer lasting, and more bizarre. Users also report that galantamine can induce the sensation of leaving the body and produce a more conscious transition from waking to dreaming while using the WBTB method. Additionally, so-called false wakings, or waking up in a dream over and over again, have been associated with galantamine use. For example, after a four-milligram dose of galantamine in combination with WBTB:

> Feeling lucid and aware, I travel outside my window and find myself waking up but soon realize it's another dream. After some time, I wake up again, only to realize it's another dream. I become aware again that I'm dreaming, yell at the sky that I want to wake up now, and finally awake in reality.

It's also common to feel galantamine's effects for several days after using it. You may also experience a delayed response, seeing little impact the night that you take galantamine but experiencing vivid lucid dreams the next day. Considering that its effects vary from person to person, its overall fast-acting quality, and its powerful ability to elicit lucid dreams, galantamine should be used with care and respect.

SIDE EFFECTS
OF USING GALANTAMINE

Though many people claim that galantamine is safe for everyone to use, this is not true.

As stated before, galantamine is a serious medication and should be taken only by those who understand the risks. Some common side effects include:

- decreased appetite
- feelings of sadness, emptiness, irritability, or ennui
- nausea or upset stomach
- trouble concentrating
- headache
- chest pain
- weakness

Symptoms of overdose include confusion, irregular breathing, severe nausea and cramping, sweating, tearing in the eyes, and muscle twitches. Seek medical attention immediately if you experience any of these. The FDA provides an excellent overview of the many potential adverse effects of galantamine. Take time to read it so that you can make an informed decision.

30
Lucid Dreaming and Technology

Technology makes our lives easier. At the same time, it also makes our lives more complicated. It has extended our waking hours into the night, allowing us to enjoy fuller, more productive modern lives; but that same benefit can also disrupt our circadian rhythms and get in the way of an active dream life. And of course, technology has now entered our dreaming life as well, with similarly mixed effects.

New lucid dreaming devices using so-called electronic lucid dream induction technology promise lucid dreams on demand. These devices use stimulating cues—a flashing light, vibration, or sound—to alert the dreamer when he or she is in REM, the hope being that the dreamer will become aware, but not awaken, and have a lucid dream. One of these gadgets, the Dreamlight, shines a bright LED into the dreamer's closed eyes; these lights often show up as a red dot within a dream. The idea is that the dreamer will learn to notice the signal and use it as a cue to become lucid.

This sounds fine at first—until we remember that REM doesn't correlate directly to dreaming. REM, as we know from research, does not necessarily mean dreaming or lucid dreaming. Even if there is some correlation, it's important to note that REM itself is hard to detect, unless you have a trained sleep specialist using electroencephalogram

(EEG) machines that cost thousands of dollars. The simpler algorithms that lucid dreaming devices use to find out if we are in REM may be wildly inaccurate. Technology has yet to develop a suitable replacement for a sleep lab when it comes to detecting REM.

Another category of devices goes beyond mere signaling cues in response to presumed REM sleep. Instead, they use electrodes to produce small electrical currents in the frontal lobe to induce lucid dreams. There is some research to support this idea, but the data itself isn't especially convincing. Further, there's the comfort factor. Whatever may be gained from using one of these devices, there's a trade-off with the discomfort of sleeping with electrodes on your forehead.

When it comes to technology to help induce lucid dreams, the best technology is still the most basic. Paper and pen (especially pens equipped with small LED lights for writing in the dark) are still the best way to record and reflect on lucid dreams. While audio cues and recorded meditations can also be effective tools, the techniques described in this book are a better way to consistently lucid dream than any technology yet developed. Personally, my list of lucid dreaming tech is pretty short:

- **A vibrating alarm clock:** I wear this on my wrist and get small vibrations based on preset alarms. I can wake up every few hours or set a time to wake up and perform WBTB.
- **A sleep mask:** This item does double duty as a sleep aid; it keeps light out, which stimulates melatonin production, and it serves as an excellent reality check. If I can see light or objects with a sleep mask on, then I can be sure I am dreaming and become lucid.
- **A phone or tablet:** A handy alternative to traditional pen and paper, ideal for when there isn't a light to write by.

That's it. No cumbersome gadgets. No potentially dangerous currents going through my brain. Just the bare minimum needed to practice awareness and recall. If you choose to take the high-tech route to practice becoming aware in dreams, that's great, but over time it's good to take off the training wheels and ride that lucid bike like a pro.

A Blessing
for the Traveler

**fully** believe that if you stay open, build your courage, and listen carefully to your dreams, you too will find the truth that your soul, your psyche, your true self, has for you. Use what you have read in this book as a guide to build your own practice. When you hear the call to adventure, accept it. Let your Hero's Journey take you where it will; trust the process. And if something I have said doesn't make sense to you, dig deeper or simply let it go. Ask your dreams for help, because they are your own ultimate resource and guide.

We have gone over many topics and techniques in this book: understanding your own psychology, using lucid dream techniques to become aware while you're dreaming, what to do while you're aware, and how to practice and come to a deeper understanding of what your dreams are communicating to you. But this is only a starting point; it is in no way a replacement for exploration into yourself.

I encourage you to read more, get other perspectives, and most importantly, to discover what works best for you. The answers you need already lie inside you. Often, we just need to do the work of the Hero's Journey. In this case, practicing lucid dreaming, meditating, and having a conversation with yourself is exactly the hard work needed.

This deep inner work, while of primary importance, is only one aspect of the worlds you are exploring. Equally important is the outside world. We are often so focused on what's inside of ourselves that we forget how important it is to explore the world that extends past our skulls. Seeing new things, discovering new cultures through travel, and meeting interesting people is a big part of being alive—and of learning more about yourself and your dreams. Engage with a community, share your dreams and insights. This is one of the most rewarding aspects of lucid dreaming. May no good story be left unshared.

Join others to talk about dreams, dreaming, and this book at taileaters.com/discussion.

Whatever journey is ahead of you, I wish you good luck and fair winds as you travel into the unknown. In your journey through dreams, I hope that you find your inner warrior, face your fears head-on, learn to love yourself, and become more aware of your place in the universe. I know you will find meaning in this process, as I have. After all, life is but a dream.

Bibliography

Adams, Lee. "Dreaming and DMT: A Connection to Psychedelic Theory." December 19, 2017, taileaters.com.

———. "How to Lucid Dream: An Easy to Follow Guide on Lucid Dreaming." January 4, 2018, taileaters.com.

Barker, Steven A., Jimo Borjigin, Izabela Lomnicka, and Rick Strassman. "LC/MS/MS Analysis of the Endogenous Dimethyltryptamine Hallucinogens, Their Precursors, and Major Metabolites in Rat Pineal Gland Microdialysate." *Biomedical Chromatography* (2013).

Barrett, Deirdre, and Patrick McNamara, eds. *The New Science of Dreaming.* Westport, Conn.: Greenwood Publishing Group, 2007.

Blavatsky, Helena Petrovna. *The Secret Doctrine: The Synthesis of Science, Religion, and Philosophy.* Pasadena, Calif.: Theosophical University Press, 2014.

Brown, David Jay. *Dreaming Wide Awake: Lucid Dreaming, Shamanic Healing, and Psychedelics.* Rochester, Vt.: Inner Traditions, 2016.

Bulkeley, Kelly. *An Introduction to the Psychology of Dreaming.* 2nd ed. Santa Barbara, Calif.: Praeger, 2017.

Burns, William E. *The Scientific Revolution: An Encyclopedia.* Santa Barbara, Calif.: ABC-CLIO, 2001.

Campbell, Joseph. *The Hero with a Thousand Faces.* Novato, Calif.: New World Library, 2008.

Chalquist, Craig. "Coming Home to a Reenchanted World." September 15, 2019. Chalquist.com.

Cooke, Sam F., and T. V. P. Bliss. "Plasticity in the Human Central Nervous System." *Brain* (July 2006).

Eliade, Mircea. *Shamanism: Archaic Techniques of Ecstasy.* Reprint edition, Princeton, N.J.: Princeton University Press, 2004.

Faraday, Ann. *The Dream Game.* New York: Harper & Row, 1990.

Francis, P. T. "Neuroanatomy/pathology and the Interplay of Neurotransmitters in Moderate to Severe Alzheimer's Disease." *Neurology, 65,* Issue 6, Supplement 3 (2005).

Freud, Sigmund, James Strachey, A. Freud, and A. Richards. *The Standard Edition of the Complete Psychological Works of Sigmund Freud.* New York: W. W. Norton, 1976.

Gordon, Amie M. "Your Sleep Cycle Revealed." *Psychology Today* blog, July 26, 2013.

Gottesmann, Claude. "GABA Mechanisms and Sleep." *Neuroscience* (2002).

Hasselmo, Michael E. "The Role of Acetylcholine in Learning and Memory." *Current Opinion in Neurobiology 16* (6) (2006).

Hobson, J. Allan. *The Dream Drugstore: Chemically Altered States of Consciousness.* Cambridge, Mass.: MIT Press, 2003.

Humble, Mats B., and Susanne Bejerot. "Orgasm, Serotonin Reuptake Inhibition, and Plasma Oxytocin in Obsessive-Compulsive Disorder. Gleaning from a Distant Randomized Clinical Trial." *Sexual Medicine 4* (3) (2016).

Hurd, Ryan. *Sleep Paralysis: A Guide to Hypnagogic Visions and Visitors of the Night.* Los Altos, Calif.: Enlightened Hyena Press, 2010.

Irwin, Lee. *The Dream Seekers: Native American Visionary Traditions of the Great Plains.* Norman: University of Oklahoma Press, 1996.

Jeffrey, Frances. "Working in Isolation: States That Alter Consensus." In B. B. Wolman and M. Ullman (eds.), *Handbook of States of Consciousness,* 249–285. New York: Van Nostrand Reinhold, 1986.

Joëls, Marian, and Harm J. Krugers. "LTP After Stress: Up or Down?" *Neural Plasticity* (2007).

Johnson, Robert A. *Inner Work: Using Dreams and Active Imagination for Personal Growth.* New York: HarperOne, 2009.

Jung, Carl Gustav. *Collected Works,* Vol. 12 and 16. Princeton, N.J.: Princeton University Press, 2014.

———. "General Aspects of Dream Psychology." In *Dreams.* Translated by R. F. C. Hull. Princeton, N.J.: Princeton University Press, 2011.

Jung, Carl Gustav, and Sonu Shamdasani, ed. *The Red Book.* New York: W. W. Norton, 2009.

Kean, Sam. *The Tale of the Dueling Neurosurgeons: The History of the Human Brain as Revealed by True Stories of Trauma, Madness, and Recovery.* New York: Little, Brown and Company, 2014.

Kihara, Takeshi, Hideyuki Sawada, Tomoki Nakamizo, Rie Kanki, Hirofumi Yamashita, Alfred Maelicke, and Shun Shimohama. "Galantamine

Modulates Nicotinic Receptor and Blocks Aβ-enhanced Glutamate Toxicity." *Biochemical and Biophysical Research Communications,* 325 (3) (2004).

Kihara, Takeshi, and Shun Shimohama. "Alzheimer's Disease and Acetylcholine Receptors." *Acta Neurobiol Exp,* 64 (1) (2004).

LaBerge, Stephen, Kristen LaMarca, and Benjamin Baird. "Pre-sleep Treatment with Galantamine Stimulates Lucid Dreaming: A Double-blind, Placebo-controlled Crossover Study." *PLOS One* (August 8, 2018).

LaBerge, Stephen, and Howard Rheingold. *Exploring the World of Lucid Dreaming.* New York: Ballantine Books, 1997.

Love, Daniel. *Are You Dreaming? Exploring Lucid Dreams: A Comprehensive Guide.* Exeter, U.K.: Enchanted Loom Publishing, 2013.

Lucidology course, Lucid Dream Forum, OBE forum on saltcube website, 2008.

Massey, Peter V., and Zafar I. Bashir. "Long-term Depression: Multiple Forms and Implications for Brain Function." *Trends in Neurosciences,* 30 (4) (2007).

Maurizi, Charles. "The Function of Dreams (REM Sleep): Roles for the Hippocampus, Melatonin, Monoamines, and Vasotocin." *Medical Hypotheses,* 23 (4) (1987).

McCarthy, Andrew, Keith Wafford, Elaine Shanks, Marcin Ligocki, Dale M. Edgar, and Derk-Jan Dijk. "REM Sleep Homeostasis in the Absence of REM Sleep: Effects of Antidepressants." *Neuropharmacology 108* (2016).

Monroe, Robert A. *Journeys Out of the Body.* New York: Harmony Books, 2014.

Mortal Mist Community. *Caffeine: The Overlooked LDS?* MortalMist.com, October 5, 2009 (no longer available).

Mu, Yangling, and Fred H. Gage. "Adult Hippocampal Neurogenesis and Its Role in Alzheimer's Disease." *Molecular Neurodegeneration,* 6 (1) (2011).

Nader, Tony. "Dr. Tony Nader - Hacking Consciousness at Stanford University, Part 1." Stanford University. YouTube. Posted by Raja Felix Kaegi. May 19, 2014.

Oudiette, Delphine, Marie-José Dealberto, Ginevra Uguccioni, Jean-Louis Golmard, Milagros Merino-Andreu, Mehdi Tafti, Lucile Garma, Sophie Schwartz, and Isabelle Arnulf. "Dreaming Without REM Sleep." *Consciousness and Cognition 21* (3) (2012).

Payne, Jessica D., and Lynn Nadel. "Sleep, Dreams, and Memory Consolidation: The Role of the Stress Hormone Cortisol." *Learning & Memory 11* (6) (2004).

Penner, Jacob, Raul Rupsingh, Matthew Smith, Jennie L. Wells, Michael J. Borrie, and Robert Bartha. "Increased Glutamate in the Hippocampus After Galantamine Treatment for Alzheimer's Disease." *Progress in Neuro-Psychopharmacology and Biological Psychiatry,* 34 (1) (2010).

Petroff, Ognen A. C. "GABA and Glutamate in the Human Brain" (Book Review). *The Neuroscientist, 8*(6) (2002).

Renzoni, Camille, ed. "Alcohol and GABA: Does Alcohol Increase GABA?" (undated article) Retrieved February 26, 2018, from therecoveryvillage website.

Restak, Richard. *Mozart's Brain and the Fighter Pilot: Unleashing Your Brain's Potential.* New York: Harmony Books, 2002.

Rogers, Naomi L., Jeanette Bowes, Kurt Lushington, and Drew Dawson. "Thermoregulatory Changes Around the Time of Sleep Onset." *Physiology & Behavior* (2009).

Sparrow, Gregory, Ryan Hurd, Ralph Carlson, and Ana Molina. "Exploring the Effects of Galantamine Paired with Meditation and Dream Reliving on Recalled Dreams: Toward an Integrated Protocol for Lucid Dream Induction and Nightmare Resolution." *Consciousness and Cognition,* 63 (August 2018): 74–88.

Steiner, Rudolph. *An Outline of Occult Science.* Scotts Valley, Calif.: CreateSpace Independent Publishing, 2011.

Stevens, Anthony. *Jung: A Very Short Introduction.* Oxford: Oxford University Press, 2001.

Stoffels, Twan. "Why Your Dreams Are Suddenly So Intense After You Stop Smoking Weed." Vice website, March 4, 2015.

Stumbrys, Tadas, Daniel Erlacher, and Peter Malinowski. "Meta-Awareness During Day and Night: The Relationship Between Mindfulness and Lucid Dreaming." *Imagination, Cognition, and Personality* (May 2015).

Turakitwanakan, Wanpen, Chantana Mekseepralard, and Panaree Busarakumtragul. "Effects of Mindfulness Meditation on Serum Cortisol of Medical Students." *J Med Assoc Thai,* 96 (1), 90th series (2013).

Waggoner, Robert. *Lucid Dreaming: Gateway to the Inner Self.* Newburyport, Mass.: Red WheelWeiser, 2008.

Wangyal, Tenzin, and Mark Dahlby, ed. *The Tibetan Yogas of Dream and Sleep.* Ithaca, N.Y.: Snow Lion Publications, 1998.

Yuschak, Thomas. *Advanced Lucid Dreaming: The Power of Supplements.* Morrisville, N.C.: Lulu Enterprises, 2006.

Zizi, Ferdinand, Girardin Jean-Louis, Clinton D. Brown, Gbenga Ogedegbe, Carla Boutin-Foster, and Samy I. McFarlane. "Sleep Duration and the Risk of Diabetes Mellitus: Epidemiologic Evidence and Pathophysiologic Insights." *Curr Diab Rep* 10 (2010): 43–47.

Zugo, Stefan. "How Guayusa Can Boost Lucid Dreams." How to Lucid website.

Index